KHIAN THAI

Thai Writing Workbook

KHIAN THAI

Thai Writing Workbook

(Second Edition)

Titima Suthiwan

RIDGE BOOKS
SINGAPORE

© Titima Suthiwan

Published under the Ridge Books imprint by:

NUS Press
National University of Singapore
AS3-01-02, 3 Arts Link
Singapore 117569

Fax: (65) 6774-0652
E-mail: nusbooks@nus.edu.sg
Website: http://nuspress.nus.edu.sg

First Edition 2006
Reprint 2006
Second Edition 2007
Reprint 2008
Reprint 2010
Reprint 2012
Reprint 2014
Reprint 2016
Reprint 2018
Reprint 2019
Reprint 2021

ISBN 978-9971-69-320-6 (Paper)

Printed by: Mainland Press Pte Ltd

Contents

Acknowledgements

I feel deeply grateful to many people who have supported me and helped make this book happen. I am indebted to Professor Edward M. Anthony, whose book, *A Programmed Course in Reading Thai Syllables* (University of Hawai'i, 1979), has been my model. I have also been inspired by the late Professor J. Marvin Brown, whose Thai language teaching materials and writings on Thai linguistics have provided me with invaluable knowledge in both areas.

This book would not have been possible without the advice and suggestions, both before and after the first draft was completed, from my students and my colleagues in the Thai language programme at the National University of Singapore.

Special thanks are due to M.R. Pongsuwan T. Bilmes, who has kindly taught me everything I know about teaching Thai; to Professor John Clark, for serving as a human guinea pig for the first draft; to Ms Sasiwimol Pratoomthin, for her admirable assistance in running the Thai language programme while this book was being written; to Dr Titima Rojkittikhun, for her invaluable assistance in the preparation of the book; to Dr Uri Tadmor, for all his editorial help; and to M.L. Sirina Jittalan, for the wonderful illustrations.

Introduction

Khian Thai is specially prepared for any Elementary Thai class where the language is initially taught with the use of phonetic symbols. It is designed to introduce to students each step in learning how to write Thai in a way the author views as the most pedagogically appropriate one, which may be different from what one will find in other books about the Thai language and its writing system. The linguistic explanations in the book may not always represent the author's own analysis of the language, but are the ones regarded as the most suitable for language learning purposes at this level.

The book is divided into two parts. In the first part, students will learn how to draw all the consonant and vowel signs, as well as tone marks, special symbols, and numerals. After that, they will move on to the second part where the writing system is presented. While this book can be used for self-study, it is particularly suited for a classroom setting, where the teacher is expected to give a lecture on each topic in class before having the students practise. The exercises provided in the book can be done either in class or at home. However, it is advisable that the teacher prepares his/her own set of exercises for classroom use, and have the students do the exercises in the book at home. Most of the exercises have two parts; A and B, each of which is the answer of the other. The students can choose to do either A or B, and check their answers from the other part. However, it will be much more beneficial for them to do both, without peeking at the answers while practising. A test should also be given from time to time, both to ensure and to improve the students' proficiency.

Even though most Thai words in this workbook are contextually meaningful, the author decided not to provide a glossary, as the objective of this workbook is strictly writing practice. However, glosses are provided in the text for the student's reference. The teacher should feel free to provide the students with the meaning of any words if the pedagogical curriculum and time allow.

Titima Suthiwan

A Note on Phonetic Transcription

The use of phonetic transcription in this book follows the system adopted by J. Marvin Brown in A.U.A. Thai Course series. The following explanation is adapted from the A.U.A. Thai Course Book 1, pp. xxii–xxiii.

Vowels

There are nine simple vowels, or monophthongs, in Standard Thai. Their phonetic symbols are presented in Table A below.

Table A: Thai simple vowels

Phonetic symbol	As in the word	Phonetic symbol	As in the word
a	father	ɔ	top
e	café	ʉ	(pronounced like u with a smile) sit
i	machine	ɛ	cat
o	home	ə	(pronounced like o with a smile) mallet
u	rude		

These vowels can occur alone or followed by the same vowel, or followed by vowel. When simple vowels are followed by the same vowel, they become long vowels (like aa). When they are followed by another vowel, they become diphthongs (like ia). Tables B and C contain examples of Thai words with all the vowels.

Table B: Short and long vowels

Vowel	Thai	Meaning	Vowel	Thai	Meaning
i	sìp	ten	ii	thii	time
e	phèt	hot, spicy	ee	lêek	number
ɛ	mɛ̀m	Ma'am	ɛɛ	khɛ̌ɛn	arm
ʉ	nʉ̀ŋ	one	ʉʉ	mʉʉ	hand
ə	ŋən	money	əə	sâə	stupid
a	fan	teeth	aa	paa	throw
u	lúk	rise	uu	hǔu	ear
o	khon	person	oo	soo	starve
ɔ	lɔ̀n	she	ɔɔ	phɔ̂ɔ	father

Table C: Diphthongs

Vowel	Thai	Meaning
ia	bia	beer
ɯa	rɯa	boat
ua	phǔa	husband

Table D contains Examples of words with the semivowels **w** and **y** as final consonants.

Table D: Words with final **w** and **y**

Vowel	Thai	Meaning	Vowel	Thai	Meaning
uy	khuy	chat	iw	hǐw	hungry
ooy	dooy	with, by	ew	rew	fast
əəy	nəəy	butter	eew	leew	bad
ɔy	thɔ̌y	back up	ɛw	thɛ̌w	row
ɔɔy	rɔ́ɔy	100	ɛɛw	mɛɛw	cat
ay	mây	not	aw	khâw	enter
aay	máay	wood	aaw	khâaw	rice
iaw	lǐaw	turn	ɯay	nɯ̀ay	tired
uay	ruay	rich			

Consonants

There are 21 consonants in Standard Thai. Table E contains examples of Thai words with these consonants along with their closest English equivalents. When two English words are given, the Thai sound is in between the two English sounds. Note that the symbol **ʔ** stands for a closing of the throat as in the middle of *uh-uh* (the English grunt meaning 'no').

Table E: Consonants

Consonant	Thai	Meaning	English	Consonant	Thai	Meaning	English
h	hɛ̌n	see	h	ʔ	ʔit	brick	it
ph	phìt	wrong	p	p	pɛ̀ɛt	eight	p-b
th	thii	time	t	t	tûu	cupboard	t-d
ch	chìit	inject	ch	c	cèt	seven	j-ch
kh	khít	think	k	k	kàt	bite	g-k
b	bɔ̀y	often	b	f	fan	teeth	f
d	duu	look at	d	s	sìi	four	s
m	mii	have	m	y	yùu	be at	y
n	nâw	rotten	n	w	wǐi	comb	w
ŋ	ŋuu	snake	sing	l	lɛ̂ɛk	exchange	l
				r	rɛ̂ɛk	first	r

Tone

There are five tones in Standard Thai. Their names and symbols, together with examples of each are given in the table below.

Table F: Tones

Name	Symbol	Thai	Meaning
Mid	*no symbol*	dii	good
Low	`	sìi	four
Falling	^	hâa	five
High	´	náam	water
Rising	ˇ	sɔ̌ɔŋ	two

PART ONE

Thai Characters

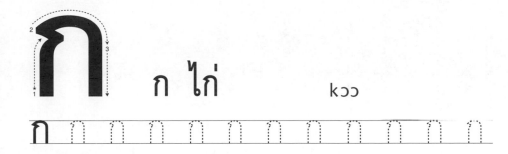

ก ไก่   kɔɔ

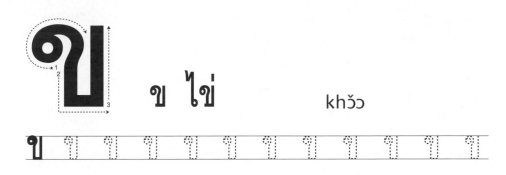

ข ไข่   khɔ̌ɔ

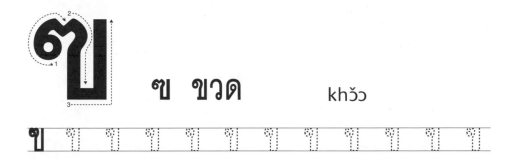

ฃ ขวด   khɔ̌ɔ

ค ควาย   khɔɔ

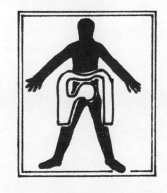

ฅ คน   khɔɔ

ฆ ระฆัง   khɔɔ

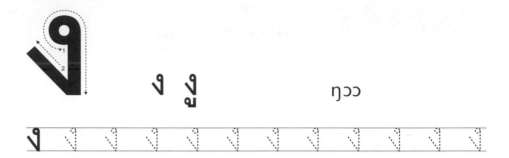

ง งู   ŋɔɔ

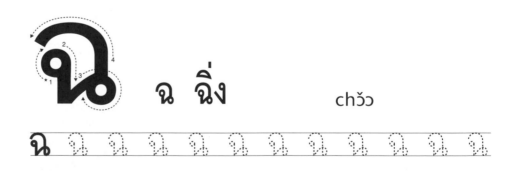

จ จาน   cɔɔ

ฉ ฉิ่ง   chɔɔ

ช ช้าง   chɔɔ

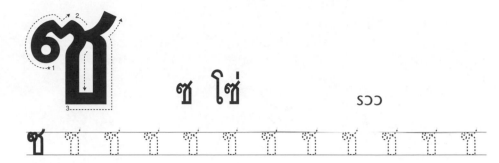

ซ โซ่   rɔɔ

ซ

ณ เณอ   chɔɔ

ณ

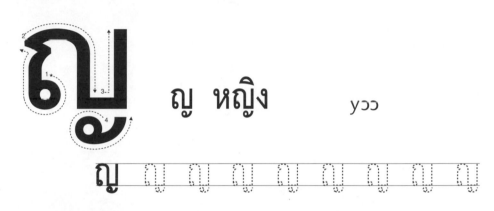

ญ หญิง   yɔɔ

ญ

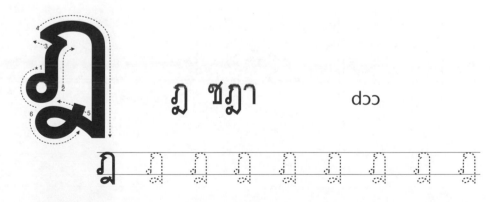

ฏ ชฎา   dɔɔ

ฏ

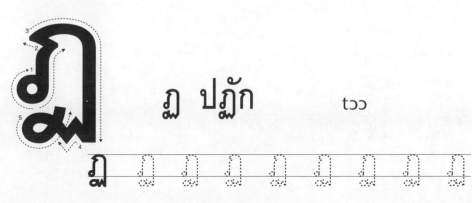

ฏ ปฏัก   tɔɔ

ฏ

5

ฐ ฐาน
ทฺว̌ว

ฑ นางมณโฑ
ทɔɔ

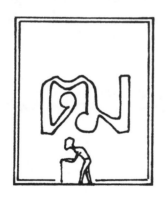

ฒ ผู้เฒ่า
ทɔɔ

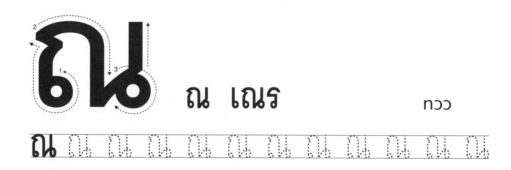

ณ เณร
นɔɔ

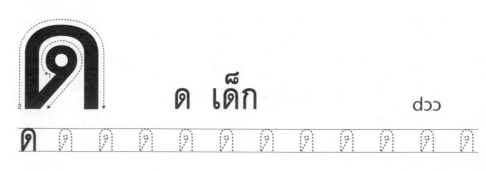

ด เด็ก
dɔɔ

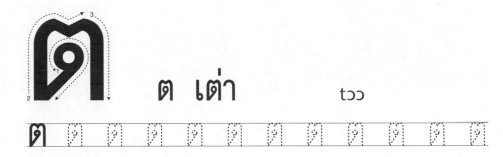

ต เต่า   tɔɔ

ต

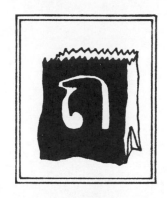

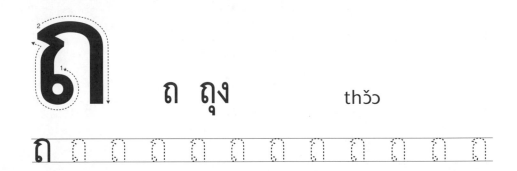

ถ ถุง   thʌ̌ɔ

ถ

ท ทหาร   thɔɔ

ท

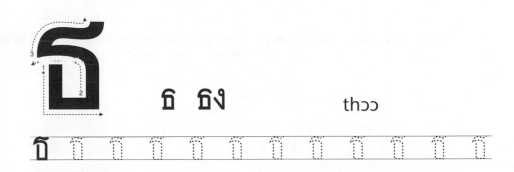

ธ ธง   thɔɔ

ธ

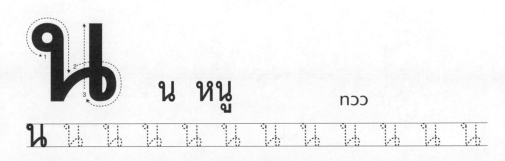

น หนู   nɔɔ

น

7

 บ ใบไม้   bɔɔ

 บ บ บ บ บ บ บ บ บ บ บ บ

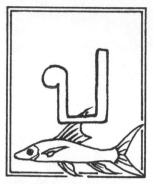
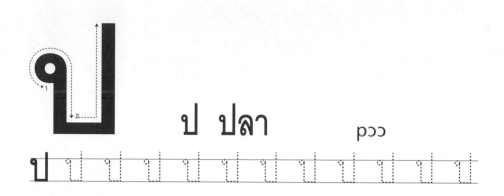
ป ปลา   pɔɔ

ป ป ป ป ป ป ป ป ป ป ป ป

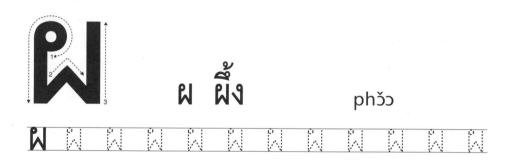
ผ ผึ้ง   phɔ̌ɔ

ผ ผ ผ ผ ผ ผ ผ ผ ผ ผ ผ ผ

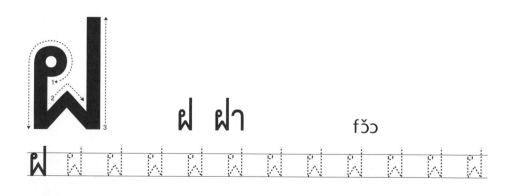
ฝ ฝา   fɔ̌ɔ

ฝ ฝ ฝ ฝ ฝ ฝ ฝ ฝ ฝ ฝ ฝ ฝ

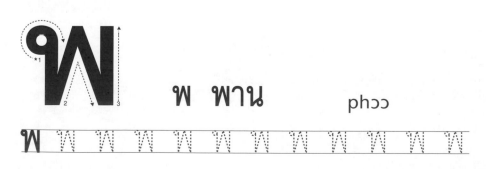
พ พาน   phɔɔ

พ พ พ พ พ พ พ พ พ พ พ พ

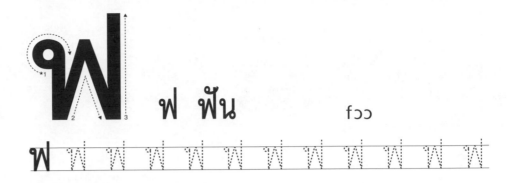

ฟ ฟัน   fɔɔ

ฟ ฟ ฟ ฟ ฟ ฟ ฟ ฟ ฟ ฟ

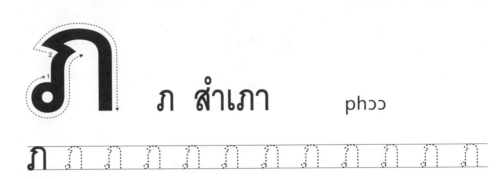

ภ สำเภา   phɔɔ

ภ ภ ภ ภ ภ ภ ภ ภ ภ ภ

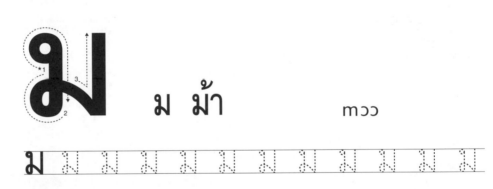

ม ม้า   mɔɔ

ม ม ม ม ม ม ม ม ม ม ม

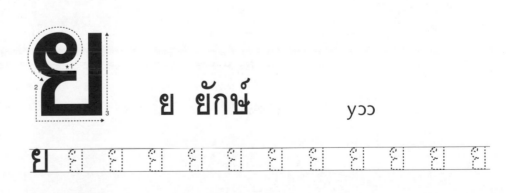

ย ยักษ์   yɔɔ

ย ย ย ย ย ย ย ย ย ย ย

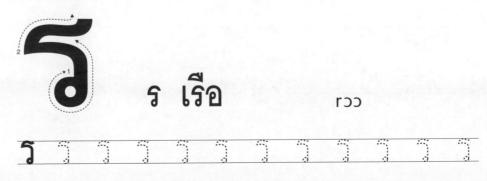

ร เรือ   rɔɔ

ร ร ร ร ร ร ร ร ร ร

ล ลิง　　　　　　　เวว

ล

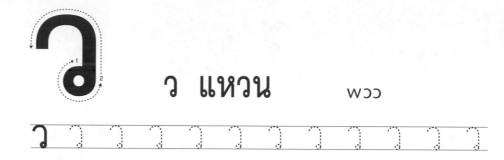

ว แหวน　　　　　พวว

ว

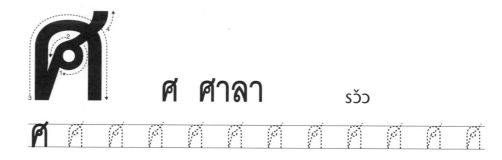

ศ ศาลา　　　　　รวว

ศ

ษ ฤๅษี　　　　　รวว

ษ

ส เสือ　　　　　　รวว

ส

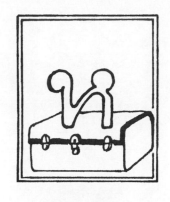

ห หีบ

หวั

ห ห ห ห ห ห ห ห ห ห ห ห

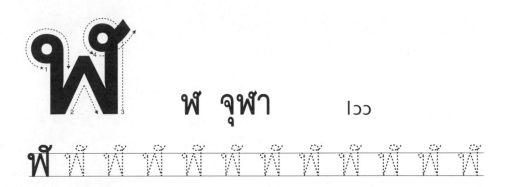

ฬ จุฬา

เวว

ฬ ฬ ฬ ฬ ฬ ฬ ฬ ฬ ฬ ฬ ฬ

อ อ่าง

ไวว

อ อ อ อ อ อ อ อ อ อ อ อ

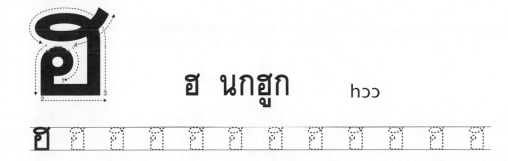

ฮ นกฮูก

ฮวว

ฮ ฮ ฮ ฮ ฮ ฮ ฮ ฮ ฮ ฮ ฮ

Vowels

a
aa

i
ii

u̶
u̶u̶

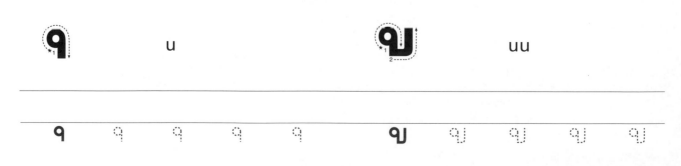

u
uu

12

e

ee

ɛ

εε

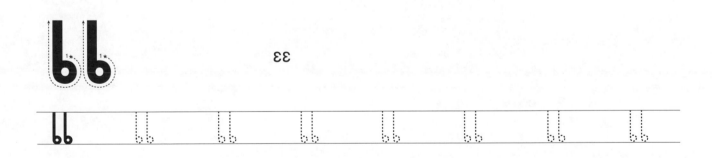

o

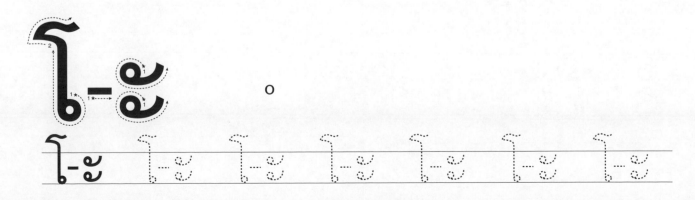

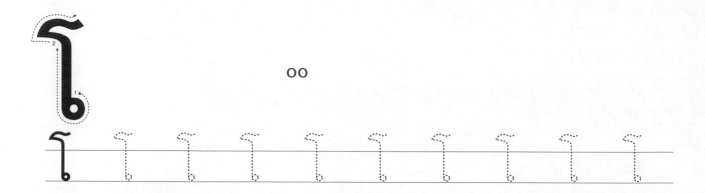

โอ

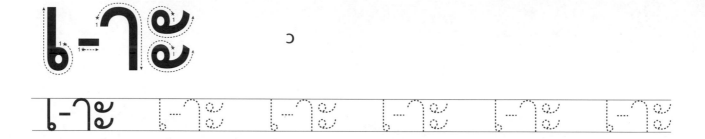

เ-าะ

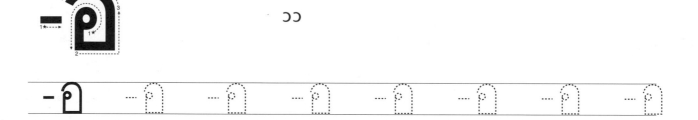

ออ

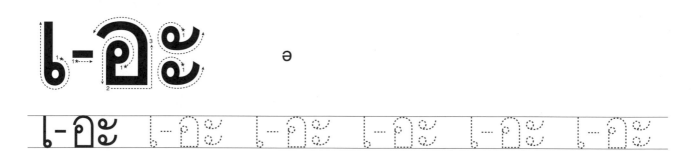

เออะ

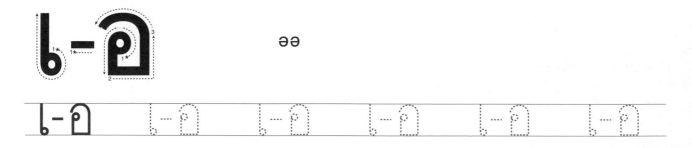

เออ

14

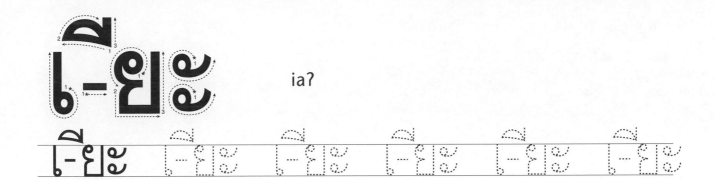

ia?

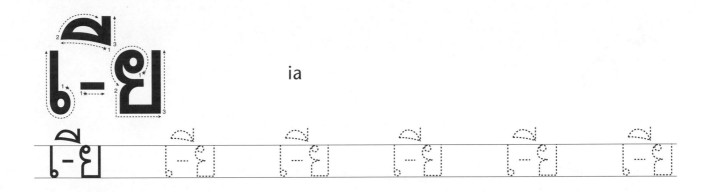

ia

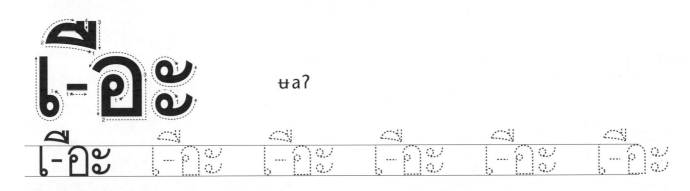

Ɬa?

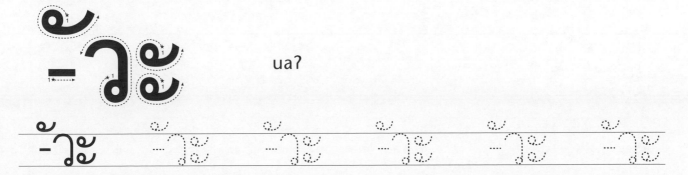

Ɬa

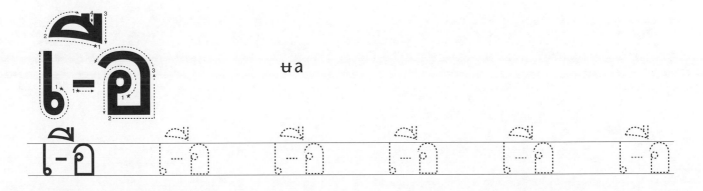

ua?

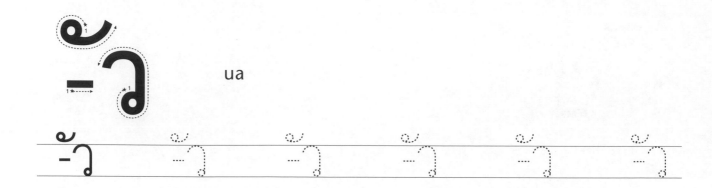

ua

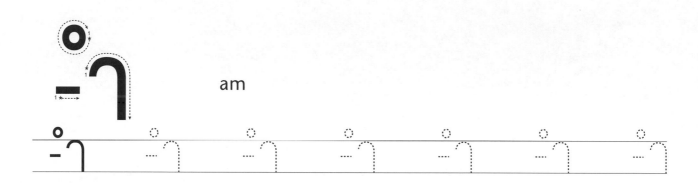

am

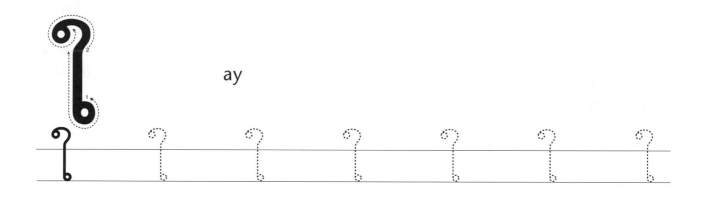

ay

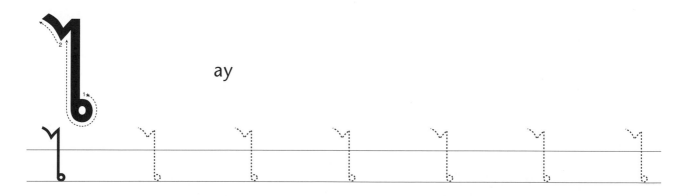

ay

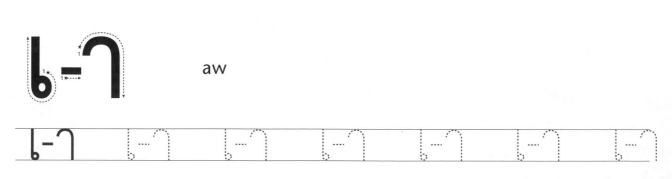

aw

16

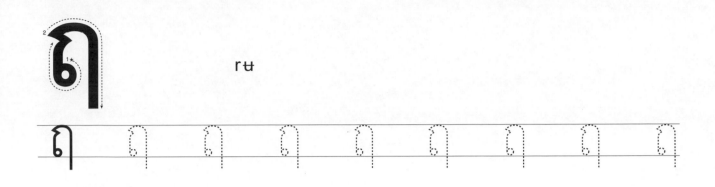

ฤๅ

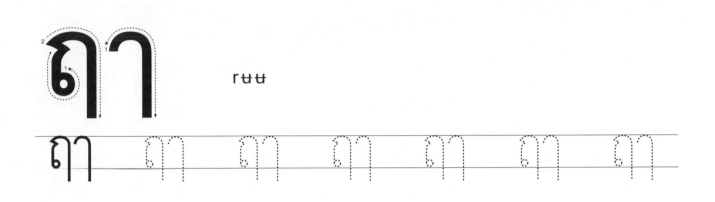

ฦๅ

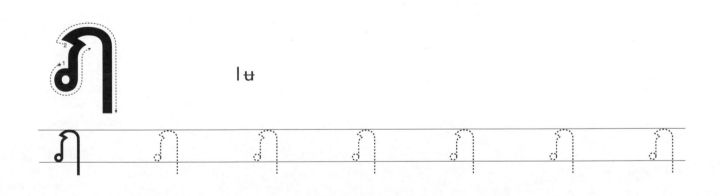

เย

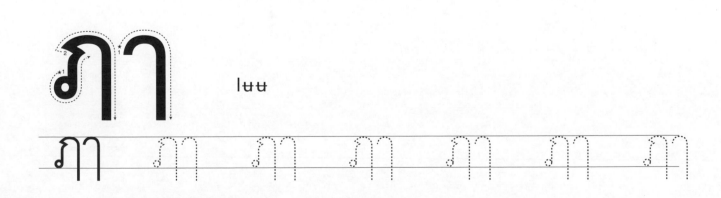

เยย

Tone Marks

Special Marks

18

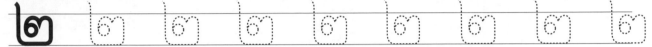

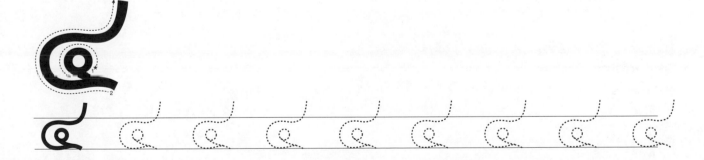

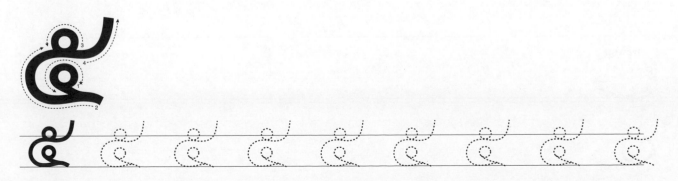

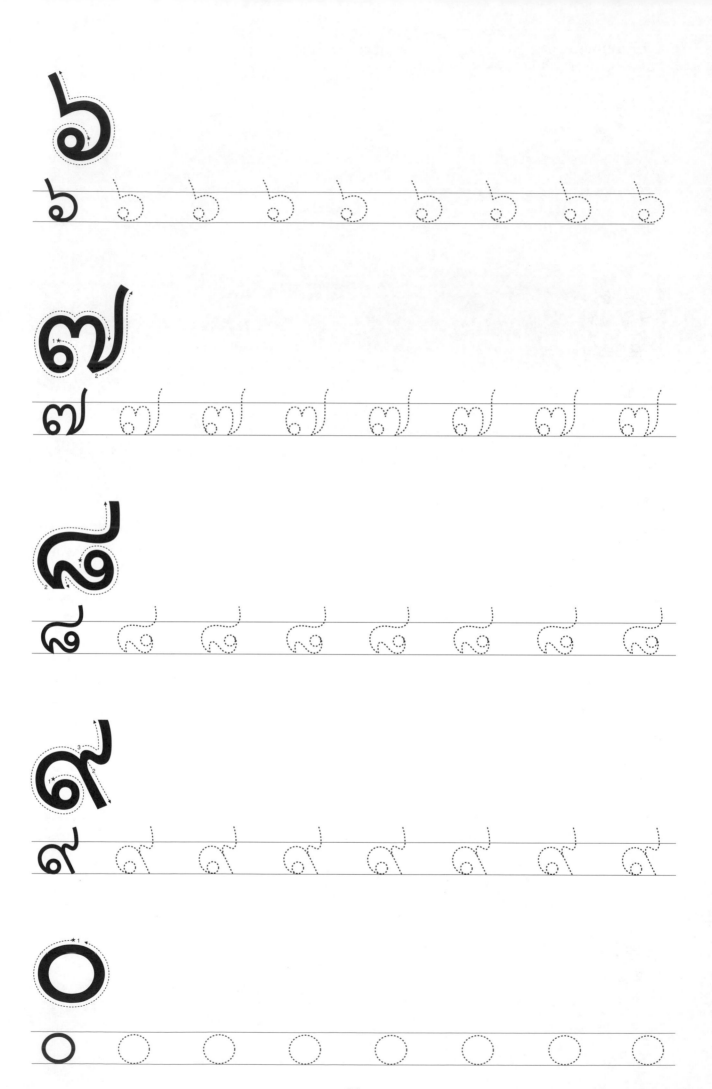

PART TWO

Thai Writing System

1. Sounds and Signs

The Sounds of Thai

Modern Standard Thai has 21 consonants and 21 vowels.[1] The consonants sounds can be conveniently divided into three groups according to their manner of articulation.[2] They are:

Plain stops:	p t k c b p ʔ
Aspirated stops, and fricatives:	ph th kh ch f s h
Sonorants:	m n ŋ y r l w

The 21 vowels are divided into 2 groups: monophthongs (simple vowels) and diphthongs (complex vowels):

Monophthongs:

- short: a   i   ɨ   u   e   ɛ   o   ɔ   ə

- long: aa   ii   ɨɨ   uu   ee   ɛɛ   oo   ɔɔ   əə

Diphthongs: ia   ɨa   ua

Thai has five distinct tones in the standard language. These tones are mid, low, falling, high, and rising.

---

[1] For further discussion, see Hudak, T.J. 1990. 'Thai', in Bernard Comrie (ed.) *The World's Major Languages*. Oxford: Oxford University Press. Pp.760-1

[2] See Brown, J.M. 1997. *A.U.A. Language Center Thai Course Reading and Writing Text mostly reading.* Ithaca: Cornell University.

The Signs of Thai

The Thai alphabet is based on the ancient Khmer and Mon scripts, which are in turn derived from southern Indian scripts used throughout Southeast Asia during the first millennium AD. These scripts were originally used to write texts in the ancient Indian languages of Sanskrit and Pali, but were later adapted to represent local languages. When the Thai alphabet was developed, additional characters were devised to represent the Thai sounds not found in Sanskrit and Pali. Symbols for Sanskrit and Pali sounds not found in Thai were kept for writing loanwords, even though they were probably pronounced with similar Thai sounds right from the start. Because of this, some sounds of Thai can be presented by different letters, depending on whether they occur in native vocabulary or in Indic loanwords.

Since 1283, when King Ramkhamhaeng of Sukhothai is said to have developed the Thai writing system[3], the spoken language has gone through numerous sound changes. For example, some voiced consonants (like *b* and *d*) became voiceless aspirates (like *ph* and *th*). Since letters already existed for *ph* and *th*, there was now yet another letter representing each of these sounds. In addition, some new tones also developed, whereas the writing system has remained largely unaltered. While new signs were added as needed to represent new sounds and tones, letters representing obsolete sounds were kept in use. Only in the 19th century were two such letters dropped from the system.

This workbook tries to introduce the Thai writing system to the students as systematically as possible. The students, for their part, should be patient with this ancient writing system. Like every language with a long history of writing, exceptions are often the best way to explain irregularities.

The students are also to note that in this book, individual syllables (which often make up complete words) are separated by spaces. In actual Thai writing, words in a clause are generally written together without any spaces, as spaces are only used to separate clauses (and hence larger units like sentences).

---

[3] This claim that King Ram Khamhaeng invented the Thai writing script appears in the inscription known as Inscription No. 1 and dated 1283 AD. Recently, some scholars questioned the authenticity of this inscription. Based on various linguistic and other factors, however, it appears to be authentic. See Chamberlain, James R. (ed.). 1991. *The Ram Khamhaeng Controversy: Collected Papers.* Bangkok: The Siam Society.

2. Thai Syllables

Thai syllables can be categorized by their **shapes** as open and closed syllables. Open syllables end with a vowel, and closed syllables end with a consonant. The followings are simple Thai syllables' canonical shapes:

1. Open syllable: CV; CVV[4]
2. Closed syllable: CVC; CVVC

A. Consonants

There are 44 consonant symbols, which from now on will be simply called 'consonants', in the Thai writing system. The ordering of these consonants is after that of the Indic script, with the insertion of the symbols designed to represent Thai sounds not found in Pali and Sanskrit. The first 33 consonants represent various types of sounds in the order of their place of articulation, and can be illustrated together in one chart. The last 11 consonants also consist of various types of sounds but not in the order of their place of articulation, and are, therefore, illustrated together in a separate chart.

Table 1: Consonant charts

Chart 1

	1		2		3		4		5	
Velar	ก	k	ข ฃ	kh	ค ค	kh	ฆ	kh	ง	ŋ
Palatal	จ	c	ฉ	ch	ช ฌ	ch s	ฌ	ch	ญ	y
Alveolar	ฎ ฏ	d t	ฐ	th	ฑ	th	ฒ	th	ณ	n
Alveolar	ด ต	d t	ถ	th	ท	th	ธ	th	น	n
Bilabial	บ ป	b p	ผ ฝ	ph f	พ ฟ	ph f	ภ	ph	ม	m

Chart 2

ย	ร	ล	ว	ศ	ษ	ส	ห	ฬ	อ	ฮ
y	r	l	w	s	s	s	h	l	ʔ	h

---

[4] C = consonant; V = vowel

25

B. Consonants groups

Thai consonants are divided into three groups according to the effect they have on the tone of each syllable.   They are:

Mid consonants: column # 1 + อ /?/

High consonants: column # 2 + ศ /s/, ษ /s/, ส /s/,ห /h/

Low consonants: column # 3, 4, 5 + ย /y/, ร /r/, ล /l/, ว /w/, ฮ /h/, ฬ /l/

C. Vowels

Vowels in Thai are categorized as simple vowels (monophthongs) and complex vowels (diphthongs). The simple vowels are further categorized as short and long vowels.

Table 2: Simple vowels (monophthongs)

	Front	Central	Back
High	i , ii	ɨ, ɨɨ	u, uu
Mid	e, ee	ə, əə	o, oo
Low	ɛ, ɛɛ		ɔ, ɔɔ
		a, aa	

Table 3: Complex vowels (diphthongs)

	Front	Central	Back
High	ia	ɨa	ua
Mid			
Low			

Table 4: Examples of Thai syllables showing vowels' length distinction:[5]

krìt	'dagger'	krìit	'to cut'	rian	'to study'
ʔen	'ligament'	ʔeen	'to recline'	rɨan	'house'
phɛ́	'goat'	phɛ́ɛ	'to be defeated'	ruan	'to be provocative'
fǎn	'to dream'	fǎan	'to slice'		
klɔ̀ŋ	'box'	klɔɔŋ	'drum'		
khôn	'thick (liquid)'	khôon	'to fell (a tree)		
sùt	'last; rearmost'	sùut	'to inhale'		
ŋən	'silver'	dəən	'to walk'		
khɨ̂n	'to go up'	khlɨ̂ɨn	'wave'		

[5] Adapted from Tingsabadh and Abramson. 1999. *Handbook of the International Phonetic Association*. UK: Cambridge University Press. P. 148

3. Mid Consonants: Initials

A. Initial consonants : C_

Table 5: Initial Mid consonants

Thai sign	Phonetic symbol	Name
ก	k	kɔɔ kày
จ	c	cɔɔ caan
ฎ[6]	d	dɔɔ chádaa
ฏ	t	tɔɔ pà tàk
ด	d	dɔɔ dèk
ต	t	tɔɔ tàw
บ	b	bɔɔ bay máay
ป	p	pɔɔ plaa
อ	ʔ	ʔɔɔ ʔàaŋ

Exercise 1A

Write the Thai consonant sign that corresponds to each name.

1. kɔɔ kày   _____

2. cɔɔ caan   _____

3. dɔɔ dèk   _____

4. tɔɔ tàw   _____

5. bɔɔ bay máay   _____

6. pɔɔ plaa   _____

7. ʔɔɔ ʔàaŋ   _____

---

[6] The relatively rare characters ฎ and ฏ will not be used at this elementary level.

Exercise 1B

Write the phonetic symbol of each Thai consonant below.

๑ . ก   ———

๒ . จ   ———

๓ . ค   ———

๔ . ต   ———

๕ . บ   ———

๖ . ป   ———

๗ . อ   ———

B. Long simple vowels: _ VV

Table 6: Long simple vowels

Thai	Phonetic symbol
—า	aa
—ี	ii
—ือ	ɯɯ
—ู	uu
เ—	ee
แ—	ɛɛ
โ—	oo
—อ	ɔɔ
เ—อ	əə

29

C. Thai syllables : C VV

k   aa   "crow', "kettle"

ก   า

Table 7: CVV

Thai	Phonetic symbol	Meaning
กา	kaa	'crow'
ตี	tii	'to hit'
ปู	puu	'crab'
แก	kɛɛ	'you, he, she, him, her'

Exercise 2A

Write the following syllables in Thai script.

1. kaa   _____   11. pii   _____

2. tii   _____   12. cɔɔ   _____

3. puu   _____   13. duu   _____

4. dii   _____   14. tɯɯ   _____

5. too   _____   15. ʔoo   _____

6. ʔaa   _____   16. cəə   _____

7. paa   _____   17. tee   _____

8. kɔɔ   _____   18. kɯɯ   _____

9. cee   _____   19. poo   _____

10. cɛɛ   _____   20. ʔəə   _____

30

Exercise 2B

Write the following syllables in phonetic symbols.

๑. กา   _____   ๑๑. ปี   _____

๒. ตี   _____   ๑๒. จอ   _____

๓. ปู   _____   ๑๓. ดู   _____

๔. ดี   _____   ๑๔. ตือ   _____

๕. โต   _____   ๑๕. โอ   _____

๖. อา   _____   ๑๖. เจอ   _____

๗. ปา   _____   ๑๗. เต   _____

๘. กอ   _____   ๑๘. กือ   _____

๙. เจ   _____   ๑๙. โป   _____

๑๐. แจ   _____   ๒๐. เออ   _____

Exercise 3A

Write the following words or sentences in Thai script.

1. taa dii   _____

2. ʔaa tii puu   _____

3. puu too   _____

4. kɨɨ cəə tɔɔ   _____

5. cɔɔ cɛɛ   _____

6. buu duu   _____

7. pii cɔɔ   _____

8. kaa taa too   _____

9. ʔaa paa pɔɔ   _____

10. kɛɛ duu dii   _____

Exercise 3 B

Write the following words or sentences in phonetic symbols.

๑. ตา ดี   _____

๒. อา ตี ปู   _____

๓. ปู โต   _____

๔. กือ เจอ ตอ   _____

๕. จอ แจ   _____

๖. บู ดู   _____

๗. ปี จอ   _____

๘. กา ตา โต   _____

๙. อา ปา ปอ   _____

๑๐. แก ดู ดี   _____

4. Low Consonants: Sonorants

Even though there are 24 Low consonants, at this level, we will learn how to write only with those in **column # 5 (nasals) + y, r, l, w,** all of which are called **sonorants**.

A. Initial sonorants: C_

Table 8: Initial sonorants

Thai	Phonetic symbol	Name
ง	ŋ	ŋɔɔ ŋuu
ญ[7]	y	yɔɔ yĭŋ
ณ	n	nɔɔ neen
น	n	nɔɔ nǔu
ม	m	mɔɔ máa
ย	y	yɔɔ yák
ร	r	rɔɔ rɰa
ล	l	lɔɔ liŋ
ว	w	wɔɔ wɛ̌ɛn

Exercise 4 A

Write the Thai consonant that corresponds with each name given below.

1. ŋɔɔ ŋuu _____

2. nɔɔ nǔu _____

3. mɔɔ máa _____

4. yɔɔ yák _____

5. rɔɔ rɰa _____

6. lɔɔ liŋ _____

7. wɔɔ wɛ̌ɛn _____

---

[7] The relatively rare characters ญ and ณ will not be used at this elementary level.

Exercise 4 B

Write the phonetic symbol of each Thai consonant below.

๑.　ง　　　———

๒.　น　　　———

๓.　ม　　　———

๔.　ย　　　———

๕.　ร　　　———

๖.　ล　　　———

๗.　ว　　　———

Exercise 5 A

Write the following syllables in Thai script.

1.　maa　———　　8.　mɯɯ　———

2.　mii　———　　9.　ruu　———

3.　ŋuu　———　　10.　laa　———

4.　yaa　———　　11.　ŋɔɔ　———

5　rɔɔ　———　　12.　ŋɛɛ　———

6.　lɛɛ　———　　13.　mee　———

7.　loo　———

35

Exercise 5 B

Write the following words or sentences in phonetic symbols.

๑. มา

_____

๒. มี

_____

๓. งู

_____

๔. ยา

_____

๕. รอ

_____

๖. แล

_____

๗. โล

_____

๘. มือ

_____

๙. รู

_____

๑๐. ลา

_____

๑๑. งอ

_____

๑๒. แง

_____

๑๓. เม

_____

36

B. Final sonorants: _ _ _ C

Table 9. Final sonorants

Thai	Phonetic symbol
ง	ŋ
น	n
ม	m
ย	y
ว	w

C. Thai syllables: C VV C

c aa n

จ า น

"plate"

Table 10: C VV C

Thai	Phonetic transcription	Meaning
กาว	kaaw	'glue'
ปีน	piin	'to climb'
เอว	ʔeew	'waist'
แดง	dɛɛŋ	'red'
ออม	ʔɔɔm	'to save'
จูง	cuuŋ	'to pull'
โกง	kooŋ	'to cheat'
ปืน	puun	'gun'
ยาว	yaaw	'to be long'
มอง	mɔɔŋ	'to look at'
ราว	raaw	'around, approximately'
ลืม	lɯɯm	'to forget'
นอน	nɔɔn	'to sleep; to lie down'
โวย	wooy	'to complain'
ตาย	taay	'to die; to be dead'

37

Exercise 6A

Write the following words or sentences in Thai script.

1. kaaŋ keeŋ   _____

2. kɔɔŋ puun   _____

3. duu daaw   _____

4. ʔeew baaŋ   _____

5. tuum taam   _____

6. ʔoon ʔeen   _____

7. paaŋ taay   _____

8. taa poon   _____

9. ciin dɛɛŋ   _____

10. doon pʉʉn   _____

11. lʉʉm mɔɔŋ   _____

12. rɔɔ naan   _____

13. wooy waay   _____

14. mooŋ yaam   _____

15. nɔɔn maa   _____

Exercise 6 B

Write the following words or sentences in phonetic symbols.

๑.   กาง เกง   ————————————

๒.   กอง ปูน   ————————————

๓.   ดู ดาว   ————————————

๔.   เอว บาง   ————————————

๕.   ตูม ตาม   ————————————

๖.   โอน เอน   ————————————

๗.   ปาง ตาย   ————————————

๘.   ตา โปน   ————————————

๙.   จีน แดง   ————————————

๑๐. โดน ปืน   ————————————

๑๑. ลืม มอง   ————————————

๑๒. รอ นาน   ————————————

๑๓ โวย วาย   ————————————

๑๔. โมง ยาม   ————————————

๑๕. นอน มา   ————————————

D. Thai syllable: CVVC, when VV is /əə/ and C# is a nasal (/n/, /ŋ/, /m/)

C VV C
d əə n

* เด อ น [8] → เดิน 'to walk'

t əə m

* เต อ ม → เติม 'to add'

E. Thai syllable: CVVC, when VV is /əə/ and C# is /y/

C VV C
l əə y

* เล อ ย → เลย 'to pass; (not) at all'

Exercise 7A

Write the following words or sentences in Thai script.

1. dəən duu daaw   _____

2. təəm puun   _____

3. taam dəəm   _____

4. kəən ləəy   _____

5. ləəy taam ləəy   _____

---

[8] An asterisk in front of a form indicates that a form which should logically occur is replaced by another form.

40

Exercise 7B

Write the following words or sentences in phonetic symbols.

๑.　เดิน ดู ดาว　　＿＿＿＿＿＿＿＿＿＿

๒.　เติม ปูน　　＿＿＿＿＿＿＿＿＿＿

๓.　ตาม เดิม　　＿＿＿＿＿＿＿＿＿＿

๔.　เกิน เลย　　＿＿＿＿＿＿＿＿＿＿

๕.　เลย ตาม เลย　　＿＿＿＿＿＿＿＿＿＿

5. Initial Mid Consonants and Short Vowels

A. Short simple vowels :

Table 11: Short simple vowels

Thai[9]	Phonetic symbol
◌ะ	**a**
◌ิ	**i**
◌ึ	**ɯ**
◌ุ	**u**
เ◌ะ	**e**
แ◌ะ	**ɛ**
โ◌ะ	**o**
เ◌าะ[10]	**ɔ**
เ◌อะ[11]	**ə**

Examples of open syllables with initial Mid consonant and a short vowel: CV

C V
c à

จะ   'will'

C V
d ù

ดุ   'to be fierce; to scold'

Note that open syllables with initial Mid consonant and a short vowel always have low tone.

---

[9] The bold forms undergo a special orthographic transformation as shown in Table 13 on page 45.

[10] Does not appear with a final consonant in words used at this elementary level.

[11] Does not appear with a final consonant in words used at this elementary level.

Below are the tone rules we have covered so far:

Table 12: Tone rules : CVV; CVVC; CVC

	Initial consonant	Vowel	Final consonant	Tone	Syllables
1.	Mid	long	----	mid	kaa
2.	Mid	long	sonorant	mid	kaaŋ
3.	Mid	short	sonorant	mid	kan
4.	**Mid**	**short**	**----**	**low**	**kà**

Exercise 8 A

Write the following words in Thai script.

1. paa   _____

2. pà   _____

3. tii   _____

4. tǐ   _____

5. kee   _____

6. tè   _____

7. duu   _____

8. dù   _____

9. tɨɨ   _____

10. tɨ̀   _____

11. kɔɔ   _____

12. kɔ̀   _____

13. poo   _____

14. pò   _____

15. kɛɛ   _____

16. kɛ̀   _____

43

Exercise 8B

Write the following words in phonetic.

๑.   ปา   ─────────

๒.   ปะ   ─────────

๓.   ตี   ─────────

๔.   ติ   ─────────

๕.   เก   ─────────

๖.   เตะ   ─────────

๗.   ดู   ─────────

๘.   ดุ   ─────────

๙.   ตือ   ─────────

๑๐. ตึ   ─────────

๑๑. กอ   ─────────

๑๒. เกาะ   ─────────

๑๓. โป   ─────────

๑๔. โปะ   ─────────

๑๕. แก   ─────────

๑๖. แกะ   ─────────

44

B. Thai syllable : CVC, when V is /a/, /e/, /o/

Table 13: /a/, /e/, /o/ + sonorants

Vowel	C V C	Thai	Meaning
a	k a n	*ก ะ น → กัน	'together'
e	p e n	*เ ป ะ น → เป็น	'to be'
o	c o n	*โ จ ะ น → จน	'to be poor; until'

Exercise 9 A

Write the following words in Thai script.

1. paan   _____

2. pan   _____

3. coon   _____

4. con   _____

5. deen   _____

6. pen   _____

7. ?aan   _____

8. ?an   _____

9. poon   _____

10. pon   _____

Exercise 9B

Write the following words in phonetic symbols.

๑. ปาน   _____

๒. ปั้น   _____

๓. โจน   _____

๔. จน   _____

๕. เดน   _____

๖. เป็น   _____

๗. อาน   _____

๘. อัน   _____

๙. โปน   _____

๑๐. ปน   _____

Exercise 10 A

Write the following phrases or sentences in Thai script.

1. maa duu puu kan _____

2. puu man dəən kὲ kà _____

3. caan bin bin maa _____

4. ʔaa kɛɛ dù _____

5. bon kɔ̀ mii kὲ _____

6. coo yiŋ pʉʉn pen _____

7. ʔaa tὲ puu con taay _____

8. baaŋ pà ʔin _____

9. dɛɛŋ kin cù _____

10. pii cɔɔ kà pii kun _____

Exercise 10B

Write the following phrases or sentences in phonetic symbols.

๑.   มา ดู ปู กัน   _____

๒.   ปู มัน เดิน เกะ กะ   _____

๓.   จาน บิน บิน มา   _____

๔.   อา แก ดุ   _____

๕.   บน เกาะ มี แกะ   _____

๖.   โจ ยิง ปืน เป็น   _____

๗.   อา เตะ ปู จน ตาย   _____

๘.   บาง ปะ อิน   _____

๙.   แดง กิน จุ   _____

๑๐.   ปี จอ กะ ปี กุน   _____

6. Final Mid Consonants

A: Final consonants: _ _ _ C

Table 14: Final Mid consonants

Thai	Phonetic symbol	
	Initial	Final
ก	k	k
จ	c	t
ด	t	t
ต[12]	t	t
บ	b	p
ป[12]	p	p
อ	ʔ	---

B. Tone rules:

Table 15. More tone rules[13]

	Initial consonant	Vowel	Final consonant	Tone	Syllables
1.	Mid	long	----	mid	kaa
2.	Mid	long	Low-sonorant	mid	kaaŋ
3.	Mid	short	Low-sonorant	mid	kan
4.	**Mid**	**short**	----	**low**	**kà**
5.	**Mid**	**short**	**Mid**	**low**	**kàk**
6.	**Mid**	**long**	**Mid**	**low**	**kàak**

---

[12] The two characters ต and ป will not be used as final consonants at this elementary level. In native Thai words, such as ones used at this level, final **t** and **p** are spelled with ด and บ respectively.

[13] These rules will be presented as part of the default tone system in lesson 7.

Exercise 11A

Write the following words in Thai script.

1. kàap   _____

2. dǐit   _____

3. cùup   _____

4. ʔɔ̀ɔp   _____

5. dàap   _____

6. tɔ̀ɔp   _____

7. pìt   _____

8. bɛ̀ɛp   _____

9. cùt   _____

10. cɯ̀ɯt   _____

Exercise 11B

Write the following words in phonetic symbols.

๑. กาบ   ————————

๒. ดีด   ————————

๓. จูบ   ————————

๔. โอบ   ————————

๕. ดาบ   ————————

๖. ตอบ   ————————

๗. ปิด   ————————

๘. แบบ   ————————

๙. จุด   ————————

๑๐. ขีด   ————————

C. Thai syllable: CVC, when V is /a/, /e/, /o/

Table 16. /a/, /e/, /o/ + oral stops

Vowel	C V C	Thai	Meaning
a	k à t	* กะด → กัด	'to bite'
e	p è t	* เปะด → เป็ด	'duck'
o	c ò t	* โจะด → จด	'to write down'

51

Exercise 12 A

Write the following words in Thai script.

1. pàt   _____

2. dèk   _____

3. cèt   _____

4. pòt   _____

5. dàp   _____

6. tòk   _____

Exercise 12 B

Write the following words in phonetic symbols.

๑. ปัด   _____

๒. เด็ก   _____

๓. เจ็ด   _____

๔. ปด   _____

๕. ดับ   _____

๖. ตก   _____

D. Thai syllable: CVVC, when VV is /əə/ and C# is an oral stop (/p/, /t/, /k/)

C VV C
k əə t

เ ก อ ด   → เกิด   'to be born; to happen, to take place'

C VV C
b əə k

เ บ อ ก   → เบิก   'to check out (something from storage); to draw (money)'

Exercise 13A
Write the following words in Thai script.

1.	pàak	_____	18.	còok	_____
2.	pàk	_____	19.	tòp	_____
3.	pìt	_____	20.	bὲɛp	_____
4.	tὲɛk	_____	21.	bǐip	_____
5.	dὲɛt	_____	22.	kèp	_____
6.	dèk	_____	23.	kàt	_____
7.	cùup	_____	24.	ʔàap	_____
8.	càp	_____	25.	ʔὲɛp	_____
9.	cǐip	_____	26.	dὕk	_____
10.	cǐp	_____	27.	cὕut	_____
11.	ʔǐik	_____	28.	còp	_____
12.	bɔ̀ɔt	_____	29.	cèp	_____
13.	bùut	_____	30.	pèt	_____
14.	còt	_____	31.	ʔòp	_____
15.	tàp	_____	32.	tɔ̀ɔp	_____
16.	pə̀ət	_____	33.	pǐik	_____
17.	dǐp	_____	34.	kɔ̀ɔt	_____

53

Exercise 13 B

Write the following words in phonetic symbols.

๑.　ปาก　———————　๑๘.　โจก　———————

๒.　ปัก　———————　๑๙.　ตบ　———————

๓.　ปิด　———————　๒๐.　แบบ　———————

๔.　แตก　———————　๒๑.　บีบ　———————

๕.　แดด　———————　๒๒.　เก็บ　———————

๖.　เด็ก　———————　๒๓.　กัด　———————

๗.　จูบ　———————　๒๔.　อาบ　———————

๘.　จับ　———————　๒๕.　แอบ　———————

๙.　จีบ　———————　๒๖.　ดึก　———————

๑๐.　จิบ　———————　๒๗.　จืด　———————

๑๑.　อีก　———————　๒๘.　จบ　———————

๑๒.　บอด　———————　๒๙.　เจ็บ　———————

๑๓.　บูด　———————　๓๐.　เปิ๊ด　———————

๑๔.　จด　———————　๓๑.　อบ　———————

๑๕.　ตับ　———————　๓๒.　ตอบ　———————

๑๖.　เปิด　———————　๓๓.　ปีก　———————

๑๗.　ดิบ　———————　๓๔.　กอด　———————

54

Exercise 14A

Write the following words or phrases in phonetic symbols.

๑.	ปาก แตก	——————	๑๑.	โบก ตึก	——————
๒.	ตาย จาก	——————	๑๒.	เปิด ปิด	——————
๓.	กอด จูบ	——————	๑๓.	ออด แอด	——————
๔.	บอบ บาง	——————	๑๔.	อาบ แดด	——————
๕.	แกง บูด	——————	๑๕.	เจ็ด แปด	——————
๖.	เตะ เจ็บ	——————	๑๖.	เปิด อบ	——————
๗.	จีบ ตอบ	——————	๑๗.	อึด ยัด	——————
๘.	กาง ปีก	——————	๑๘.	ตา บอด	——————
๙.	แบก ปืน	——————	๑๙.	เติบ โต	——————
๑๐.	เบิก ปูน	——————	๒๐.	จืด จาง	——————

Exercise 14 B

Write the following words or phrases in Thai script.

1. pàak tɛ̀ɛk   _____

2. taay càak   _____

3. kɔ̀ɔt cùup   _____

4. bɔ̀ɔp baaŋ   _____

5. kɛɛŋ bùut   _____

6. tè cèp   _____

7. cìip tɔ̀ɔp   _____

8. kaaŋ pǐik   _____

9. bɛ̀ɛk pɨɨn   _____

10. bə̀ək puun   _____

11. bòok tɨk   _____

12. pə̀ət pìt   _____

13. ʔɔ̀ɔt ʔɛ̀ɛt   _____

14. ʔàap dɛ̀ɛt   _____

15. cèt pɛ̀ɛt   _____

16. pèt ʔɔ̀p   _____

17. ʔɨt ʔàt   _____

18. taa bɔ̀ɔt   _____

19. tə̀əp too   _____

20. cɨɨt caaŋ   _____

Exercise 15 A

Write the following phrases or sentences in phonetic symbols.

๑.   ตา ดู อา จับ ปู บน เกาะ   _____

๒.   ตา บอก อา เป็น เด็ก จัง   _____

๓.   อา แอบ กิน แกง ปู อัด กับ กะ ปิ   _____

๔.   แกะ บุก แบก แดด ตอน ดึก   _____

๕.   ลา ตา บอด กิน เป็ด อบ   _____

๖.   เด็ก เด็ก เดิน กอด กัน เกะ กะ   _____

๗.   ยาย มี ยา กัน ปาก แตก   _____

๘.   มือ ยาย บอบ บาง จัง   _____

๙.   จาน บิน จาก ดาว แดง ตก   _____

๑๐.   ตา ลืม รอ ยาย   _____

๑๑.   จูน โบก มือ ลา จอน   _____

๑๒   จน ตาย จาก กัน   _____

Exercise 15 B

Write the following words in Thai script.

1. taa duu ʔaa càp puu bon kɔ̀   _____

2. taa bɔ̀ɔk ʔaa pen dèk caŋ   _____

3. ʔaa ʔɛ̀ɛp kin puu ʔàt kàp kà pǐ   _____

4. kɛ̀ bùk bɛ̀ɛk dɛ̀ɛt tɔɔn dὺk   _____

5. laa taa bɔ̀ɔt kin pèt ʔɔ̀p   _____

6. dèk dèk dəən kɔ̀ɔt kan kɛ̀ kà   _____

7. yaay mii yaa kan pàak tɛ̀ɛk   _____

8. mὺὺ yaay bɔ̀ɔp baaŋ caŋ   _____

9. caan bin càak daaw dɛɛŋ tòk   _____

10. taa lὺὺm rɔɔ yaay   _____

11. cuun bɔ̀ɔk mὺὺ laa cɔɔn   _____

12. con taay càak kan   _____

58

7. Tones in Standard Thai:
Default tones

A. Live and Dead syllables

Syllables in Thai are divided according to their **sounds** into two categories: live syllable and dead syllable. Live syllables are open syllables with a long vowel, and closed syllables with a final sonorant. Dead syllables are open syllables with a short vowel, and closed syllables with a final oral stop[14].

Table 17: Live and Dead syllables

Live syllable	Dead syllable
CVV กา	**CV** จะ
CVC (ŋ, m, n, w, y) กิน	**CVC (p, t, k)** ปิด
CVVC (ŋ, m, n, w, y) จาน	**CVVC (p, t, k)** ปาก

B. Default tones

Because Thai is a tonal language, each syllable must have a tone. When no tone marker is used, an automatic default tone is assigned by the quality of its vowel and its initial and final consonants. Table 18 presents the default tone of each type of Thai syllables.

---

14 It is important to note here that open syllables with a short vowel and closed syllables with a final oral stop are grouped together under the dead syllable category because open syllables with a short vowel end in a phonetic glottal stop, /ʔ/, unless immediately followed by another stop.

Table 18: Default tones in Thai[15]

Initial consonant	Live		Dead	
	Long vowel	**Short vowel**	**Long vowel**	**Short vowel**
Mid	mid กา kaa	mid กิน kin	low กาบ kàap	low กับ kàp
High	rising ขา khǎa	rising ขัน khǎn	low ขาด khàat	low ขัด khàt
Low	mid มา maa	mid มัน man	falling มาก mâak	high มัก mák

---

[15] Exercises in this lesson will cover only syllables with initial Mid and Low consonants, as initial High consonants will be introduced in a later lesson.

Exercise 16A

Write the following syllables in phonetic symbols.

๑.	ปา	——————	๑๑.	มด	——————
๒.	กัด	——————	๑๒.	มืด	——————
๓.	บิน	——————	๑๓.	วัด	——————
๔.	ลาก	——————	๑๔.	รอด	——————
๕.	ลง	——————	๑๕.	ลาบ	——————
๖.	วัน	——————	๑๖.	มุก	——————
๗.	มิด	——————	๑๗.	รบ	——————
๘.	วืด	——————	๑๘.	แนบ	——————
๙.	รัก	——————	๑๙.	มอบ	——————
๑๐.	จืด	——————	๒๐.	รับ	——————

61

Exercise 16 B

Write the following syllables in Thai script.

1. paa   _____
2. kàt   _____
3. bin   _____
4. lâak   _____
5. loŋ   _____
6. wan   _____
7. nít   _____
8. wûut   _____
9. rák   _____
10. cùut   _____
11. mót   _____
12. mûut   _____
13. wát   _____
14. rôɔt   _____
15. lâap   _____
16. múk   _____
17. róp   _____
18. nɛ̂ɛp   _____
19. mɔ̂ɔp   _____
20. ráp   _____

8. More on Low consonants

There are altogether 24 Low consonants, 7 of which have been covered in the previous lessons. One consonant, ฅ, is now obsolete because the sound it represented does not exist in Modern Standard Thai. Table 19 illustrates all low consonants in the current orthography in initial and final positions.

Note that letters in the shaded boxes will not be included in the exercises in this lesson because they appear less often in the Thai language at the elementary level. Due to the same pedagogical reason, Low consonants other than ง น ม ย ว will not be used at the final position. At this stage, only ก ด บ are used for /k/, /t/, and /p/ respectively at final position.

Table 19: Low consonants

| Thai sign | | Phonetic symbol | |
Letter	Name	Initial	Final
ค	khɔɔ khwaay	kh	k
ฅ	khɔɔ rá khaŋ	kh	k
ง	ŋɔɔ ŋuu	ŋ	ŋ
ช	chɔɔ cháaŋ	ch	t
ซ	sɔɔ sôo	s	t
ฌ	chɔɔ chəə	ch	t
ญ	yɔɔ yĭŋ	y	n
ฑ	thɔɔ mon thoo	th/d	t
ฒ	thɔɔ phûu thâw	th	t
ณ	nɔɔ neen	n	n
ท	thɔɔ thá hǎan	th	t
ธ	thɔɔ thoŋ	th	t
น	nɔɔ nǔu	n	n
พ	phɔɔ phaan	ph	p
ฟ	fɔɔ fan	f	p
ภ	phɔɔ sǎm phaw	ph	p
ม	mɔɔ máa	m	m
ย	yɔɔ yák	y	y
ร	rɔɔ rɰa	r	n
ล	lɔɔ liŋ	l	n
ว	wɔɔ wɛ̌ɛn	w	w
ฬ	lɔɔ cùlaa	l	n
ฮ	hɔɔ nók hûuk	h	-

64

Exercise 17A

Write the Thai consonant that corresponds to each name given below.

1.   khɔɔ khwaay   _____

2.   chɔɔ cháaŋ   _____

3.   sɔɔ sôo   _____

4.   thɔɔ thá hǎan   _____

5.   phɔɔ phaan   _____

6.   fɔɔ fan   _____

7.   hɔɔ nók hûuk   _____

Exercise 17B

Write the phonetic symbol of each Thai consonant below as used in initial position.

๑.   ค   _____

๒.   ช   _____

๓.   ซ   _____

๔.   ฑ   _____

๕.   พ   _____

๖.   ฟ   _____

๗.   ฮ   _____

Exercise 18 A

Write the following Live syllables in Thai script.

1. khuu   _____

2. thii   _____

3. phaa   _____

4. chaa   _____

5. soo   _____

6. fɔɔŋ   _____

7. hee   _____

8. khan   _____

9. thɛɛn   _____

10. chaam   _____

11. phaŋ   _____

12. faŋ   _____

13. fɛɛn   _____

14. khɨɨ   _____

15. khəəy   _____

66

Exercise 18B

Write the following Live syllables in phonetic symbols.

๑. คู
_____

๒. ที
_____

๓. พา
_____

๔. ชา
_____

๕. โซ
_____

๖. ฟอง
_____

๗. เฮ
_____

๘. คัน
_____

๙. แทน
_____

๑๐. ชาม
_____

๑๑. พัง
_____

๑๒. ฟัง
_____

๑๓. แฟน
_____

๑๔. คือ
_____

๑๕. เคย
_____

Exercise 19A

Write the following Dead syllables in phonetic symbols.

๑. คะ

_____

๒. คิด

_____

๓. พบ

_____

๔. ชัด

_____

๕. ชอบ

_____

๖. พูด

_____

๗. รัก

_____

๘. ลัก

_____

๙. นะ

_____

๑๐. นิด

_____

๑๑. นอก

_____

๑๒. แยก

_____

๑๓. ซอก

_____

๑๔. และ

_____

๑๕. วาด

_____

Exercise 19B

Write the following Dead syllables in Thai script.

1. khá   _____

2. khít   _____

3. phóp   _____

4. chát   _____

5. chɔ̂ɔp   _____

6. phûut   _____

7. rák   _____

8. lák   _____

9. ná   _____

10. nít   _____

11. nɔ̂ɔk   _____

12. yɛ̂ɛk   _____

13. sɔ̂ɔk   _____

14. lɛ́   _____

15. wâat   _____

Exercise 20A

Write the following sentences in Thai script.

1. cee pen khon ciin

_____

2. cim maa càak haa waay

_____

3. nít phóp rák

_____

4. fɛɛn núk chɔ̂ɔp kin pèt

_____

5. yaay dəən maa wát thúk wan

_____

6. taa phûut daŋ mâak

_____

Exercise 20 B

Write the following sentences in phonetic symbols.

๑. เจ เป็น คน จีน

_____

๒. จิม มา จาก ฮา วาย

_____

๓. นิด พบ รัก

_____

๔. แฟน นุก ชอบ กิน เป็ด

_____

๕. ยาย เดิน มา วัด ทุก วัน

_____

๖. ตา พูด ดัง มาก

_____

70

9. High Consonants

There are 11 High consonants as illustrated in the table below.

Table 20. High consonants

| Thai sign | | Phonetic symbol | |
Letter	Name	Initial	Final
ข	khɔ̌ɔ khày	kh	k
ฃ [16]	khɔ̌ɔ khùat	kh	k
ฉ	chɔ̌ɔ chìŋ	ch	t
ฐ	thɔ̌ɔ sǎn thǎan	th	t
ถ	thɔ̌ɔ thǔŋ	th	t
ผ	phɔ̌ɔ phûŋ	ph	p
ฝ	fɔ̌ɔ fǎa	f	p
ศ	sɔ̌ɔ sǎa laa	s	t
ษ	sɔ̌ɔ rɨɨ sǐi	s	t
ส	sɔ̌ɔ sɨ̌a	s	t
ห	hɔ̌ɔ hìip	h	-

Note that letters in the shaded boxes will not be included in the exercises in this lesson because they appear less often in the Thai language at the elementary level. Due to the same pedagogical reason, no High consonants will be used at the final position.

---

[16] This letter is no longer in use.

71

Exercise 21A

Write the Thai consonant that corresponds with each name given below.

1. khɔ̌ɔ khày   _____

2. chɔ̌ɔ chìŋ   _____

3. sɔ̌ɔ sǔa   _____

4. thɔ̌ɔ thǔŋ   _____

5. phɔ̌ɔ phûŋ   _____

6. fɔ̌ɔ fǎa   _____

7. hɔ̌ɔ hìip   _____

Exercise 21B

Write the phonetic symbol of each initial Thai consonant below.

๑. ข   _____

๒. ฉ   _____

๓. ส   _____

๔. ถ   _____

๕. ผ   _____

๖. ฝ   _____

๗. ห   _____

Exercise 22A

**Write the following Live syllables in phonetic symbols. Refer to Table 18, page 60
for the tone.**

๑.   ขา   _____

๒.   ถาม   _____

๓.   แผน   _____

๔.   โฉม   _____

๕.   สอง   _____

๖.   ฝอย   _____

๗.   หาว   _____

๘.   ขัง   _____

๙.   ถุง   _____

๑๐.   ฉัน   _____

๑๑.   ผม   _____

๑๒.   ฝัน   _____

๑๓.   สิง   _____

๑๔.   เห็น   _____

๑๕.   เฉย   _____

๑๖.   ถึง   _____

Exercise 22B

Write the following Live syllables in Thai script. Refer to Table 18, page 60 for the tone.

1. khǎa   _____

2. thǎam   _____

3. phěɛn   _____

4. chǒom   _____

5. sǒɔŋ   _____

6. fɔ̌ɔy   _____

7. hǎaw   _____

8. khǎŋ   _____

9. thǔŋ   _____

10. chǎn   _____

11. phǒm   _____

12. fǎn   _____

13. sǐŋ   _____

14. hěn   _____

15. chǎəy   _____

16. thǔŋ   _____

At this point, you may have noticed that some Low consonant **signs** representing **non-sonorant sounds** have High consonants counterparts, as illustrated in the table below.

Table 21: Corresponding Low and High consonants.

Sound	Low consonant		High consonant	
	Sign	**Name**	**Sign**	**Name**
kh	ค	khɔɔ	ข	khɔ̌ɔ
ch	ช	chɔɔ	ฉ	chɔ̌ɔ
s	ซ	sɔɔ	ส	sɔ̌ɔ
th	ท	thɔɔ	ถ	thɔ̌ɔ
ph	พ	phɔɔ	ผ	phɔ̌ɔ
f	ฟ	fɔɔ	ฝ	fɔ̌ɔ
h	ฮ	hɔɔ	ห	hɔ̌ɔ
ŋ	ง	ŋɔɔ	-	-
n	น	nɔɔ	-	-
m	ม	mɔɔ	-	-
y	ย	yɔɔ	-	-
r	ร	rɔɔ	-	-
l	ล	lɔɔ	-	-
w	ว	wɔɔ	-	-

75

Exercise 23 A

Write the following syllables in Thai script. Refer to Table 18, page 60 for the tone.

1. khɛɛn   _____

2. khɛ̌ɛn   _____

3. chəəy   _____

4. chə̌əy   _____

5. sɔɔy   _____

6. sɔ̌ɔy   _____

7. hee   _____

8. hě̌e   _____

9. thuy   _____

10. thǔy   _____

11. phɛɛŋ   _____

12. phɛ̌ɛŋ   _____

13. faŋ   _____

14. fǎŋ   _____

Exercise 23B

Write the following syllables in phonetic symbols. Refer to Table 18, page 60 for the tone.

๑.　แคน　　　　＿＿＿＿＿＿

๒.　แขน　　　　＿＿＿＿＿＿

๓.　เชย　　　　＿＿＿＿＿＿

๔.　เฉย　　　　＿＿＿＿＿＿

๕.　ซอย　　　　＿＿＿＿＿＿

๖.　สอย　　　　＿＿＿＿＿＿

๗.　เฮ　　　　＿＿＿＿＿＿

๘.　เห　　　　＿＿＿＿＿＿

๙.　ทุย　　　　＿＿＿＿＿＿

๑๐.　ถุย　　　　＿＿＿＿＿＿

๑๑.　แพง　　　　＿＿＿＿＿＿

๑๒.　แผง　　　　＿＿＿＿＿＿

๑๓.　ฟัง　　　　＿＿＿＿＿＿

๑๔.　ฝัง　　　　＿＿＿＿＿＿

10. Initial High Consonants in Dead Syllables

The previous lesson covered initial High consonants in Live syllables. In this lesson, initial High consonants in Dead syllables will be covered. In order to do so, however, it would be helpful to review the default tones of syllables with initial High consonants.

Table 22: Initial High consonants and default tones

Initial consonant	Live		Dead	
	Long vowel	Short vowel	Long vowel	Short vowel
High	rising ขา khǎa	rising ขัน khǎn	low ขาด khàat	low ขัด khàt

Exercise 24A

Write the following syllables in phonetic symbols.

๑. ขูด   _____

๒. ฉีด   _____

๓. สิบ   _____

๔. หก   _____

๕. หัก   _____

๖. ถูก   _____

๗. ฝืด   _____

๘. ขับ   _____

๙. ผิด   _____

๑๐. แฝด   _____

78

Exercise 24B

Write the following syllables in Thai script.

1. khùut   _____

2. chǐit   _____

3. sǐp   _____

4. hòk   _____

5. hàk   _____

6. thùuk   _____

7. fɯ̀ɯt   _____

8. khàp   _____

9. phǐt   _____

10. fɛ̀ɛt   _____

Exercise 25A

Write the following sentences in phonetic symbols.

๑. จิม มี ลูก สาว สอง คน   อา ยุ สิบ แปด ปี กับ สิบ หก ปี

_____

๒. นก สี ขาว ปีก หัก ตก ลง มา จาก ตึก

_____

๓. วัน แรก จอน มา สาย

_____

๔. ตา ชอบ กิน กบ ผัด เผ็ด กับ แกง จืดมาก

_____

๖. ฉัน นอน ดึก ทุก คืน

_____

79

Exercise 25B

Write the following sentences in Thai script.

1. cim mii lûuk săaw sɔ̌ɔŋ khon   ʔaa yú sìp pὲɛt pii kàp sìp hòk pii

_____

2. nók sĭi khăaw pìik hàk tòk loŋ maa càak tὺk

_____

3. wan rêɛk cɔɔn maa săay

_____

4. taa chɔ̂ɔp kin kòp phàt phèt kàp kɛɛŋ cὺ̴ut mâak

_____

5. chăn nɔɔn dὺk thúk khɯɯn

_____

11. Special High consonants

Table 21 in Lesson 9 shows 7 Low consonant sounds that have corresponding High consonant sounds. The signs, or letters, of the two groups are different. Together, they constitute the first half of the table. The second half contains 7 Low sonorant sounds that do not have **distinctively different** corresponding High sonorant **signs,** even though such sounds exist. They are written with the letter ห in the front, and appear only at the **initial** position.

Table 23. High sonorants

Sound	Low sonorant		High sonorant	
	Sign	**Name**	**Sign**	**Name**
ŋ	ง	ŋɔɔ	หง	-
n	น	nɔɔ	หน	-
m	ม	mɔɔ	หม	-
y	ย / ญ	yɔɔ	หย /หญ	-
r	ร	rɔɔ	หร	-
l	ล	lɔɔ	หล	-
w	ว	wɔɔ	หว	-

These High sonorants undergo the same default tone rules as the other High consonants.

Exercise 26A

Write the following Live syllables in phonetic symbols.

๑. หนา _____

๒. แหวน _____

๓. หมู _____

๔. หวาน _____

๕. หรู _____

๖. หลาน _____

๗. หรือ _____

๘. เหรอ _____

๙. หยิม _____

๑๐. หนุน _____

๑๑. หนาว _____

๑๒. แหนม _____

๑๓. หนี _____

๑๔. แหย _____

๑๕. หลา _____

๑๖. โหล _____

๑๗. โหยง _____

๑๘. หมุน _____

๑๙. หมัน _____

๒๐. เหมื่น _____

Exercise 26B

Write the following Live syllables in Thai script.

1. nǎa   _____

2. wɛ̌ɛn   _____

3. mǔu   _____

4. wǎan   _____

5. rǔu   _____

6. lǎan   _____

7. rǔɯ   _____

8. rǎə   _____

9. yǐm   _____

10. nǔn   _____

11. nǎaw   _____

12. nɛ̌ɛm   _____

13. nǐi   _____

14. yɛ̌ɛ   _____

15. lǎa   _____

16. lǒo   _____

17. yǒoŋ   _____

18. mǔn   _____

19. mǎn   _____

20. mɛ̌n   _____

Exercise 27A

Write the following sentences in Thai script.

1. lǎan khǎay mǔu wǎan

_____

2. nǔu nǎaw thúk wan

_____

3. cim chɔ̂ɔp mǎa rǔɰ mɛɛw khá

_____

4. chǎn mii wɛ̌ɛn lǎay woŋ

_____

5. luŋ cəə lûuk mǐi lǒŋ thaaŋ

_____

Exercise 27B

Write the following sentences in phonetic symbols.

๑. หลาน ขาย หมู หวาน

_____

๒. หนู หนาว ทุก วัน

_____

๓. จิม ชอบ หมา หรือ แมว คะ

_____

๔. ฉัน มี แหวน หลาย วง

_____

๕. ลุง เจอ ลูก หมี หลง ทาง

_____

Exercise 28A

Write the following Dead syllables in phonetic symbols.

๑. หมาก

๒. หยอด

๓. หมัด

๔. หยุด

๕. หลุด

๖. หลอก

๗. หวัด

๘. หงิก

๙. หมึก

๑๐. เหน็บ

๑๑. หลับ

๑๒. หนืด

๑๓. หวาด

๑๔. หนัก

๑๕. หยิก

Exercise 28B

Write the following Dead syllables in Thai script.

1. màak   _____

2. yɔ̀ɔt   _____

3. màt   _____

4. yùt   _____

5. lùt   _____

6. lɔ̀ɔk   _____

7. wàt   _____

8. ŋìk   _____

9. mùk   _____

10. nèp   _____

11. làp   _____

12. nùut   _____

13. wàat   _____

14. nàk   _____

15. yìk   _____

Exercise 29A

Write the following sentences in phonetic symbols

๑. ฝน ตก หนัก

_____

๒. เด็ก เด็ก เป็น หวัด หมด ทุก คน

_____

๓. จิม มี ปาก กา หมึก แดง ขาย

_____

๔. ผม จอน หยิก หวี ยาก

_____

๕. หนู แหวน ขา เป็น เหน็บ

_____

Exercise 29B

Write the following sentences in Thai script.

1. fŏn tòk nàk

_____

2. dèk dèk pen wàt mòt thúk khon

_____

3. cim mii pàak kaa mùk dɛɛŋ khǎay

_____

4. phǒm cɔɔn yìk   wǐi yâak

_____

5. nǔu wɛ̌ɛn khǎa pen nèp

_____

12. Tones and Tone Marks in Standard Thai

A. Tones

There are **five** tones in spoken Thai, as illustrated in the table below.

Table 24. Tones in spoken Thai

Tone	Phonetic symbol
mid	no phonetic symbol
low	`
falling	^
high	´
rising	ˇ

B. Tones marks

In the written language, there are **four** tone marks. They are used to mark the **non-default tones.**

Table 25. Tone marks in Thai

Tone mark		Symbol[17]
Name	Meaning	
máay ʔèek	the first mark	'
máay thoo	the second mark	๗
máay trii	the third mark	๘
máay càttàwaa	the fourth mark	+

As the default tones of all types of Thai syllables have already been covered, this lesson will present the non-default tones and their marks. Table 26 in the following page illustrates the whole tonal and tone marking system in Thai.

---

[17] It is helpful to note here the similarity of these signs and the numeral used in English, i.e. ' and 1, ๗ and 2, ๘ and 3 , and + and 4.

88

C. Tonal and tone marking system

Table 26. Tones and tone marks in Standard Thai

Syllable	Tone				
	mid	**low**	**falling**	**high**	**rising**
Initial Mid consonant					
Live	กา	ก่า	ก้า	ก๊า	ก๋า
	กัน	กั่น	กั้น	กั๊น	กั๋น
Dead	–	ก่ะ >กะ	ก้ะ	ก๊ะ	*ก๋ะ
	–	ก่าก >กาก	ก้าก	ก๊าก	*ก๋าก
Initial High consonant					
Live	–	ข่า	ข้า	–	ขา
	–	ขั่น	ขั้น	–	ขัน
Dead	–	ข่ะ >ขะ	ข้ะ	–	–
	–	ข่าก >ขาก	ข้าก	–	–
Initial Low consonant					
Live	คา	–	ค่า	ค้า	–
	คัน	–	คั่น	คั้น	–
Dead	–	–	ค่ะ	ค้ะ > คะ	–
	–	–	ค่าก >คาก	ค้าก	–

Notes to Table 26: Tone and tone marking rules

1. There is no intrinsic relationship between the tones and the tone marks.
2. In each group of initial consonants, mark the live syllables first.
3. Syllables with a **default tone** do not take a tone mark, as it would be redundant.
3. After the default tone, tones to be marked are in the order of low, falling, high, and rising.
4. The marking of any dead syllables is after that of their live counterpart.

Exercise 30

Write the following syllables in phonetic symbols.

๑.   กา   ——————   ๑๑.   รัก   ——————

๒.   ขา   ——————   ๑๒.   จ๋ำ   ——————

๓.   คา   ——————   ๑๓.   สาม   ——————

๔.   กับ   ——————   ๑๔.   หมา   ——————

๕.   ขับ   ——————   ๑๕.   กั้น   ——————

๖.   คับ   ——————   ๑๖.   มั่น   ——————

๗.   บ้า   ——————   ๑๗.   หมั้น   ——————

๘.   ข้า   ——————   ๑๘.   น่า   ——————

๙.   ค่า   ——————   ๑๙.   หน้า   ——————

๑๐.   กั๊ก   ——————   ๒๐.   ซ่า   ——————

13. Initial Mid Consonants and Tone marks

A. Live syllables

Live syllables that begin with a Mid consonant can bear all <u>five tones</u>, and can be written with all <u>four tone marks</u>.

kaa	kàa	kâa	káa	kǎa
กา	ก่า	ก้า	ก๊า	ก๋า

ʔɔɔn	ʔɔ̀ɔn	ʔɔ̂ɔn	ʔɔ́ɔn	ʔɔ̌ɔn
ออน	อ่อน	อ้อน	อ๊อน	อ๋อน

pum	pùm	pûm	púm	pǔm
ปุม	ปุ่ม	ปุ้ม	ปุ๊ม	ปุ๋ม

Exercise 31

Complete each line by writing the other four tone or tone mark combinations for each consonant-vowel sequence.

1. baan
   บาน _____ _____ _____ _____

2. kuŋ
   กุง _____ _____ _____ _____

3. cim
   จิม _____ _____ _____ _____

4. dii
   ดี _____ _____ _____ _____

5. ton
   ตน _____ _____ _____ _____

Exercise 32A

Write the following words or phrases in Thai script.

1. taa tóo too   _____

2. kìi pii   _____

3. bùm bàam   _____

4. cǔm cǐm   _____

5. kǎa kàn   _____

6. dɔ̀ɔk kɛ̂ɛw   _____

7. tàaŋ daaw   _____

8. dùɯm kɔ̀ɔn   _____

9. taam túɯ   _____

10. dûɯ dâan   _____

11. pen bâa   _____

12. tǒo těe   _____

13. puun pân   _____

14. tòk bɔ̀ɔ   _____

15. kin kûŋ   _____

16. kôo kěe   _____

17. kooy ʔâaw   _____

18. ʔɔ̀ɔt ʔɔ̂ɔn   _____

19. kâam puu   _____

20. tôn tɔɔ   _____

92

Exercise 32B

Write the following words or phrases in phonetic symbols.

๑. ตา โต๊ โต   ————   ๑๑. เป็น บ้า   ————

๒. กี่ ปี   ————   ๑๒. โต๋ เต๋   ————

๓. บุ่ม บ่าม   ————   ๑๓. ปูน ปั้น   ————

๔. จุ๋ม จิ๋ม   ————   ๑๔. ตก บ่อ   ————

๕. ก๋า กั่น   ————   ๑๕. กิน กุ้ง   ————

๖. ดอก แก้ว   ————   ๑๖. โก้ เก๋   ————

๗. ต่าง ดาว   ————   ๑๗. โกย อ้าว   ————

๘. ดื่ม ก่อน   ————   ๑๘. ออด อ้อน   ————

๙. ตาม ตื๊อ   ————   ๑๙. ก้าม ปู   ————

๑๐. ดื้อ ด้าน   ————   ๒๐. ต้น ตอ   ————

B. Dead Syllables

Dead syllables that begin with a Mid consonant can bear <u>three tones</u>, and can be written with <u>two tone marks</u>

cà	câ	cá		kàap	kâap	káap
จะ	จ้ะ	จ๊ะ		กาบ	ก้าบ	ก๊าบ

tò	tô	tó		còɔt	côɔt	cóɔt
โตะ	โต้ะ	โต๊ะ		จอด	จ้อด	จ๊อด

tùk	tûk	túk
ตุก	ตุ้ก	ตุ๊ก

93

Exercise 33

Complete each line by writing the other four tone or tone mark combinations for each consonant-vowel sequence.

1. càak _____ _____

   จาก _____ _____

2. p̆iip _____ _____

   ปีบ _____ _____

3. cùut _____ _____

   จูด _____ _____

4. càp _____ _____

   จับ _____ _____

5. ʔòp _____ _____

   อบ _____ _____

Exercise 34 A
Write the following words or phrases in Thai script.

1.	túk kɛɛ	_____	6.	cúp c̆ip	_____
2.	c̃iŋ còk	_____	7.	tûp tâp	_____
3.	dɛɛŋ péɛt	_____	8.	cá cǎa	_____
4.	tòk tó	_____	9.	cɔ́ cɛ́	_____
5.	c̆iit cáat	_____	10.	kɔ́ cók toŋ	_____

94

Exercise 34 B

Write the following words or phrases in phonetic symbols.

๑.   ตุ๊ก แก   _____

๒.   จิ้ง จก   _____

๓.   แดง แป๊ด   _____

๔.   ตก โต๊ะ   _____

๕.   จี๊ด จ๊าด   _____

๖.   จุ๊บ จิ๊บ   _____

๗.   ตุ้บ ตั้บ   _____

๘.   จ๊ะ จ๋ำ   _____

๙.   เจ๊าะ แจ๊ะ   _____

๑๐.   โก๊ะ จ๊ก ตง   _____

95

14. Initial High Consonants and Tone marks

A. Live syllables

Live syllables that begin with a High consonant can bear <u>three tones</u>, and can be written with <u>two tone marks</u>.

khǎa	khàa	khâa
ขา	ข่า	ข้า

hɔ̌ɔm	hɔ̀ɔm	hɔ̂ɔm
หอม	ห่อม	ห้อม

mǎn	màn	mân
หมัน	หมั่น	หมั้น

Exercise 35
Complete each line by writing the other four tone or tone mark combinations for each consonant-vowel sequence.

1. hǐw   _____   _____

    หิว   _____   _____

2. sɔɔn   _____   _____

    สอน   _____   _____

3. lǒn   _____   _____

    หลน   _____   _____

4. nǎa   _____   _____

    หนา   _____   _____

5. thǎa   _____   _____

    ถา   _____   _____

Exercise 36A

Write the following phrases or sentences in Thai script.

1.   nâa nǎaw tôoŋ hòm phâa nǎa   _____

2.   sôm lòn bon lǎŋ mǔu   _____

3.   hǐw khâaw rʉ̌ʉ yaŋ khá   _____

4.   nâa tàaŋ pen fâa   _____

5.   tὲεŋ ŋaan pen fàŋ pen fǎa   _____

Exercise 36B

Write the following phrases or sentences in phonetic symbols.

๑.   หน้า หนาว ต้อง ห่ม ผ้า หนา   _____

๒.   ส้ม หล่น บน หลัง หมู   _____

๓.   หิว ข้าว หรือ ยัง คะ   _____

๔.   หน้า ต่าง เป็น ฝ้า   _____

๕.   แต่ง งาน เป็น ฝั่ง เป็น ฝา   _____

B. Dead Syllables[18]

Dead syllables that begin with a High consonant can bear <u>two tones</u>, and can be written with <u>only one tone mark</u>

khà	khâ		khàap	khâap
ขะ	ข้ะ		ขาบ	ข้าบ

phàk	phâk		mòt	môt
ผัก	ผั้ก		หมด	หมั้ด

Exercise 37

Complete each line by writing the other four tone or tone mark combinations for each consonant-vowel sequence.

1. khàat _____

    ขาด _____

2. là _____

    หละ _____

3. nàk _____

    หนัก _____

4. yɔ̀ɔt _____

    หยอด _____

5. wɛ̀ɛk _____

    แหวก _____

---

[18] Most of the syllables with the **non-default** tone in this category (dead syllables with High consonant initial) are meaningless.

15. Initial Low Consonants and Tone Marks.

A. Live syllables

Live syllables that begin with a Low consonant can bear <u>three tones</u>, and can be written with <u>two tone marks</u>.

khaa	khâa	kháa
คา	ค่า	ค้า

muŋ	mûŋ	múŋ
มุง	มุ่ง	มุ้ง

sɔɔn	sɔ̂ɔn	sɔ́ɔn
ซอน	ซ่อน	ซ้อน

Exercise 38

Complete each line by writing the other four tone or tone mark combinations for each consonant-vowel sequence.

1. laa   _____   _____

    ลา   _____   _____

2. phɔɔ   _____   _____

    พอ   _____   _____

3. ruu   _____   _____

    รู   _____   _____

4. thɛɛŋ   _____   _____

    แทง   _____   _____

5. hee   _____   _____

    เฮ   _____   _____

Exercise 39A

Write the following phrases or sentences in Thai script.

1. phɔ̂ɔ rúu wâa mɛ̂ɛ chɔ̂ɔp mɛɛw   _____

2. wan níi chán yûŋ tháŋ wan   _____

3. bâan lăŋ nán nâa rák mâak   _____

4. mii máa nâŋ nâa bâan   _____

5. nɔ́ɔŋ nɔɔn lɛ́ɛw ná cá   _____

Exercise 39B

Write the following phrases or sentences in phonetic symbols.

๑. พ่อ รู้ ว่า แม่ ชอบ แมว   _____

๒. วัน นี้ ฉัน ยุ่ง ทั้ง วัน   _____

๓. บ้าน หลัง นั้น น่า รัก มาก   _____

๔. มี ม้า นั่ง หน้า บ้าน   _____

๕. น้อง นอน แล้ว นะ จ๊ะ   _____

B. Dead Syllables[19]

Dead syllables that begin with a Low consonant can bear <u>two tones</u>, and can be written with <u>only one tone mark</u>

khá	khâ		khâat	kháat
คะ	ค่ะ		คาด	ค้าด

mák	mâk		mâak	máak
มัก	มั่ก		มาก	ม้าก

phút	phût		phûut	phúut
พุด	พุ่ด		พูด	พู้ด

Exercise 40

Complete each line by writing the other four tone or tone mark combinations for each consonant-vowel sequence.

1. lá   _____

    ละ   _____

2. sí   _____

    ซิ   _____

3. chɔ̂ɔp   _____

    ชอบ   _____

4. nɛ́   _____

    แนะ   _____

5. yɯ̂ɯt   _____

    ยืด   _____

---

[19] Most of the syllables with the **non-default** tone in this category (dead syllables with Low consonant initial) are meaningless.

Exercise 41A

Write the following phrases or sentences in Thai script.

1. lέεw chăn lâ   _____

2. ʔâa pàak sî   _____

3. thá lee lúk   _____

4. fáa lêεp lέ fáa róɔŋ   _____

5. phûut cháa cháa nɔ̀ɔy   _____

Exercise 41B

Write the following phrases or sentences in phonetic symbols.

๑. แล้ว ฉัน ล่ะ   _____

๒. อ้า ปาก ซิ   _____

๓. ทะ เล ลึก   _____

๔. ฟ้า แลบ และ ฟ้า ร้อง   _____

๕. พูด ช้า ช้า หน่อย   _____

16. Consonant Clusters

A cluster is a sequence of consonants with no intervening vowels. In modern Standard Thai, there are 11 consonant cluster sounds. They are: /kr/, /kl/, /kw/, /khr/, /khl/, /khw/, /pr/,/pl/, /phr/, /phl/, and /tr/. These consonant clusters appear at syllable initial position and the tone of the syllable is determined by the first consonant. Table 27 contains examples of actual Thai words with clusters.

Table 27: Consonant cluster sounds and signs

Sound	Sign	Words	Phonetic symbol	Meaning
kr	กร	กรุง	kruŋ	'big city'
kl	กล	กล้อง	klɔ̂ɔŋ[20]	'camera'
kw	กว	กวาง	kwaaŋ	'deer'
khr	ขร	ขรม	khrǒm	'to be noisy, up roaring'
	คร	ครู	khruu	'teacher'
khl	ขล	โขลง	khlǒoŋ	'a herd'
	คล	คลอง	khlɔɔŋ	'canal'
khw	ขว	ขวา	khwǎa	'right hand side'
	คว	ควาย	khwaay	'water buffalo'
pr	ปร	แปร	prɛɛ	'to change'
pl	ปล	แปล	plɛɛ	'to translate'
phr	พร	พระ	phrá	'monk'
phl	พล	เพลง	phleeŋ	'song'
tr	ตร	ตรง	troŋ	'to be straight'

---

[20] In actual pronunciation, the vowel in this word gets shortened, thus /klɔ̂ŋ/.

Exercise 42A
Write the following words in phonetic symbols.

๑.   พรม   ——————   ๑๑.   ปลอบ   ——————

๒.   กรอง   ——————   ๑๒.   ตรม   ——————

๓.   คล้อง   ——————   ๑๓.   แพรว   ——————

๔.   กว้าง   ——————   ๑๔.   พร้าว   ——————

๕.   แขวน   ——————   ๑๕.   พลอง   ——————

๖.   ความ   ——————   ๑๖.   แคล้ว   ——————

๗.   ขวาน   ——————   ๑๗.   คลาด   ——————

๘.   ขลุม   ——————   ๑๘.   พราก   ——————

๙.   ขริบ   ——————   ๑๙.   เพราะ   ——————

๑๐. ปลอม   ——————   ๒๐.   คลั่ง   ——————

104

Exercise 42B
Write the following words in Thai script.

1. phrom _____
2. krɔɔŋ _____
3. khlɔ́ɔŋ _____
4. kwâaŋ _____
5. khwɛ̆ɛn _____
6. khwaam _____
7. khwǎan _____
8. khlǔm _____
9. khr̆ip _____
10. plɔɔm _____

11. plɔ̀ɔp _____
12. trom _____
13. phrɛɛw _____
14. phráaw _____
15. phlɔɔŋ _____
16. khlɛ́ɛw _____
17. khlâat _____
18. phrâak _____
19. phrɔ́ _____
20. khlâŋ _____

17. Diphthongs

There are three diphthongs, or complex vowels, in Thai. They are /ia/, /ɨa/, and /ua/. Some linguists distinguish between short and long diphthongs. In this book, only long diphthongs are treated, as in reality short diphthongs appear only in onomatopoeia, nicknames, and Chinese loanwords[21].

A. /ia/, /ɨa/

Table 28: Diphthongs : /ia/, /ɨa/

Sound	Sign	Words	Phonetic symbol	Meaning
ia	เ ◌ ย	เตี้ย	tîa	'to be short'
		เสียง	sǐaŋ	'sound'
ɨa	เ ◌ อ	เกลือ	klɨa	'salt'
		เดือน	dɨan	'month'

B. /ua/

Table 29: Diphthong: /ua/

Sound	Sign		Words	Phonetic symbol	Meaning
	Syllable	Form			
ua	CV	◌ ว	ตัว	tua	'body'
	CVC	_ว_	นวด	nûat	'to massage'

See, however, section C on page 111.

Exercise 43A
Write the following words in Thai script.

1. phiaŋ   _____
2. phŭan   _____
3. klua   _____
4. khrua   _____
5. tɨan   _____
6. rian   _____
7. rɯ̂aŋ   _____
8. chuan   _____
9. ŋûaŋ   _____
10. bɯ̀a   _____

11. bua   _____
12. sĭa   _____
13. rɯ̂ay   _____
14. pɯ̀ay   _____
15. r̃iak   _____
16. thûa   _____
17. thùa   _____
18. chiaŋ   _____
19. lɯ́ay   _____
20. khĭaw   _____

107

Exercise 43B
Write the following words in phonetic symbols.

๑. เพียง ————— ๑๑. บัว —————

๒. เพื่อน ————— ๑๒. เสีย —————

๓. กลัว ————— ๑๓. เรื่อย —————

๔. ครัว ————— ๑๔. เปื่อย —————

๕. เตือน ————— ๑๕. เรียก —————

๖. เรียน ————— ๑๖. ทั่ว —————

๗. เรื่อง ————— ๑๗. ถั่ว —————

๘. ชวน ————— ๑๘. เชียง —————

๙. ง่วง ————— ๑๙. เลื้อย —————

๑๐. เบื่อ ————— ๒๐. เขียว —————

108

Exercise 44A
Write the following phrases or sentences in phonetic symbols.

๑. จิม ชอบ พูด เรื่อย เจื้อย น่า เบื่อ มาก

_____

๒. นี่ คือ เคียว เกี่ยว ข้าว นะ คะ

_____

๓. งู เหลือม เลื้อย เชื่อง ช้า

_____

๔. ม้า เพรียว วิ่ง เที่ยว ทั่ว ท้อง ทุ่ง

_____

๕. คอย เดี๋ยว นะ ครับ

_____

๖. ขอ ก๋วย เตี๋ยว เนื้อ หนึ่ง ชาม

_____

๗. ช่วย เปิด ประ ตู หน่อย

_____

๘. พี่ น้อง บ้าน นี้ ร้อง เพลง เพราะ ทุก คน

_____

๙. ผม กับ เพื่อน ที่ ชื่อ เพลิน มา จาก เชียง ราย

_____

๑๐.นัก เรียน ง่วง นอน เพราะ ครู พูด ช้า มาก

_____

Exercise 44B

Write the following phrases or sentences in Thai script.

1. cim chɔ̂ɔp phûut rûay cûay nâa bùa mâak

_____

2. nĩi khɯɯ khiaw kìaw khâaw ná khá

_____

3. ŋuu lŭam lúay chûaŋ cháa

_____

4. máa phriaw wîŋ thîaw thûa thɔ́ɔŋ thûŋ

_____

5. khɔɔy dǐaw ná khráp

_____

6. khɔ̌ɔ kǔay tǐaw núa nɯ̀ŋ chaam

_____

7. chûay pə̀ət pràtuu nɔ̀ɔy

_____

8. phĩi nɔ́ɔŋ bâan nĩi rɔ́ɔŋ phleeŋ phrɔ́ thúk khon

_____

9. phŏm kàp phɯ̂an thĩi chɯ̂ɯ phləən maa càak chiaŋ raay

_____

10. nák rian ŋûaŋ nɔɔn phrɔ́ khruu phûut cháa mâak

_____

C. Note on Onomatopoeia and Chinese loanwords.

Onomatopoeia is the formation of phonetic sounds that reflect sounds in the external world, like *buzz, murmur,* and *cuckoo* in English. Table 30 contains examples of onomatopoeia and Chinese loanwords in Thai with the so called 'short diphthongs'. Note that since such words in Thai are all open syllables, /ʔ/ and ะ are therefore used to represent the 'shortness' quality of the vowels in phonetic representation and Thai writing respectively. Tone assignment for these syllables follows the tone rules for Dead syllables in each initial consonant category.

Table 30: Onomatopoeia and Chinese loanwords.

Words	Phonetic symbol	Meaning
เผียะ	pʰìaʔ	'a slapping sound'
ผัวะ	pʰùaʔ	'a sound of whipping or slapping'
ยั้วะ	yúaʔ	'to get mad' (slang)
เกี๊ยะ	kíaʔ	'wooden sandals, wooden clogs'
เจี๊ยะ	cíaʔ	'to eat' (slang)

111

18. Special Vowel Forms

You might have noticed, when practicing writing closed syllables with the short vowel /a/ in earlier lessons, that the final consonants of those syllables were always /p/, /t/, /k/, /ŋ/, and /n/. The three other possible final consonants, /m/, /y/ and /w/, never appeared in the exercises. This is because syllables that end with one of these consonant sounds are **usually** written with special signs. Those special signs are also regarded by Thai grammarians as vowel signs, even though from a modern linguistic perspective they contain a consonant. Table 31 illustrates these special forms, in comparison with the expected ones.

Table 31: Special vowel signs

Vowel + m, y, w	Expected sign	Special sign	Name	Words	Phonetic symbols	Meaning
am	ั ม	ำ	sàrà ʔam	ทำ	tham	'to do; to make'
ay	ั ย	ไ_	sàrà ʔay máay malay	ไป	pay	'to go'
		ใ_	sàrà ʔay máay múan	ให้	hây	'to give'
aw	ั ว	เ_า	sàrà ʔaw	เรา	raw	'we, us'

A. /am/

Most Thai syllables ending in /am/ are written with sàrà ʔam (ำ). Those that are written with the expected sign (ั ม) tend to be Indic and recent loanwords, and will not appear in exercises in this lesson.

B. /ay/

As shown in Table 31, there are two special signs for this one vowel. Historically, they were used to represent two different vowel sounds that apparently got merged into one, i.e. /ay/. The only way, for Thais and foreigners alike, to know when to write ไ_ and ใ_ is by memorizing the only 20 words that are written with the latter. They are as shown in Table 32.

Table 32: sàrà ʔay máay múan

	Thai	Phonetic symbol	Meaning
๑ .	ใจ	cay	'heart'
๒ .	ใด	day	'any; what'
๓ .	ใบ	bay	'leaf'
๔ .	ใคร	khray	'who'
๕ .	ใน	nay	'in'
๖ .	ใย	yay	'fiber'
๗ .	ใฝ่	fày	'to be fond of'
๘ .	ใส่	sày	'to put in; to put on'
๙ .	ใหญ่ [22]	yày	'to be big'
๑๐ .	ใหม่	mày	'to be new'
๑๑ .	ใกล้	klây	'near'
๑๒ .	ใต้	tâay	'under'
๑๓ .	ใบ้	bây	'to be mute; to signal'
๑๔ .	ใคร่	khrây	'to desire'
๑๕ .	ใช่	chây	'yes'
๑๖ .	ให้	hây	'to give'
๑๗ .	ใช้	cháy	'to use'
๑๘ .	สะใภ้	sàpháy	'a female in-law'
๑๙ .	ใส	sǎy	'to be clear'
๒๐ .	หลงใหล	lǒŋlǎy	'to be infatuated'

Any other words with the vowel /ay/ are **always** written with ไ_ Examples of such words are shown in Table 33 below.

---

[22] Note that this word is spelt with หญ , not หย .

113

Table 33: sàrà ʔay máay malay

Thai	Phonetic symbol	Meaning
ไก่	kày	'chicken'
ไกล	klay	'far'
ไต	tay	'kidney'
ไต่	tày	'to climb'
ไฟ	fay	'fire'
ไฝ	fǎy	'mole'
ไส	sǎy	'to shove, to push'
ไหม	mǎy	'silk'
ไหม้	mây	'to burn'
ไม่	mây	'no; not'

Like **/am/**, certain words are written with the expected sign ◌ั ย. These words tend to be Indic and recent loans and will not appear in exercises in this lesson.

C. /aw/

Logically, following the writing convention of a closed syllable with a short vowel /a/, ◌ัว should be the way to write **/aw/**. However, since the sign เ◌า was taken from Khmer to represent **/aw/**, so ◌ัว was free to represent **/ua/** in an open syllable (refer to Table 29)

Table 34: sàrà ʔaw

Thai	Phonetic symbol	Meaning
เสา	saw	'pole'
เงา	ŋaw	'shadow'
เหงา	ŋǎw	'to be lonely'
เดา	daw	'to guess'

114

Exercise 45 A

Write the following words or phrases in Thai script.

1. kham   _____

2. nam   _____

3. pay   _____

4. lám   _____

5. ʔaw   _____

6. tôm yam   _____

7. khày kày   _____

8. phâa mǎy   _____

9. sôm tam   _____

10. cay dii   _____

11. klay   _____

12. klây   _____

13. maw lâw   _____

14. khǎm   _____

15. fay mây   _____

16. thîi nǎy   _____

17. tây din   _____

18. klày klia   _____

19. kam ray   _____

20. ʔà ray   _____

Exercise 45 B

Write the following words or phrases in phonetic symbols.

๑. คำ   _____   ๑๑. ไกล   _____

๒. นำ   _____   ๑๒. ใกล้   _____

๓. ไป   _____   ๑๓. เมา เหล้า   _____

๔. ล้ำ   _____   ๑๔. ขำ   _____

๕. เอา   _____   ๑๕. ไฟ ไหม้   _____

๖. ต้ม ยำ   _____   ๑๖. ที่ ไหน   _____

๗. ไข่ ไก่   _____   ๑๗. ใต้ ดิน   _____

๘. ผ้า ไหม   _____   ๑๘. ไกล่ เกลี่ย _____

๙. ส้ม ตำ   _____   ๑๙. กำ ไร   _____

๑๐. ใจ ดี   _____   ๒๐. อะ ไร   _____

116

Exercise 46A
Write the following phrases or sentences in phonetic symbols.

๑. ใคร ขาย ไข่ ไก่

_____

๒. ไหม ใหม่ ไม่ ไหม้

_____

๓. เทียน ไข ของ ใคร

_____

๔. จด หมาย หาย ไป ไหน

_____

๕. ปลา ใหญ่ กิน ปลา เล็ก

_____

๖. นี่ ข้าว หน้า ไก่ ไม่ ใช่ ข้าว ผัด

_____

๗. คิด ใหม่ ทำ ใหม่

_____

๘. มี อะ ไร ใน ใจ

_____

๙. เริด ร้าง ห่าง ไกล

_____

๑๐. บ้าน ใกล้ เรือน เคียง

_____

Exercise 46B

Write the following phrases or sentences in Thai script.

1. khray khǎay khày kày

_____

2. mǎy mày mây mây

_____

3. thian khǎy khɔ̌ɔŋ khray

_____

4. còt mǎay hǎay pay nǎy

_____

5. plaa yày kin plaa lék

_____

6. ñii khâaw nâa kày mây chây khâaw phàt

_____

7. khít mày tham mày

_____

8. mii ʔàray nay cay

_____

9. rɘ̂ɘt ráaŋ hàaŋ klay

_____

10. bâan klây rɥan khiaŋ

_____

19. The Regular Irregulars

A number of commonly used Thai are grouped together under this topic because they either have an unusual written form, or have a written form that does not match the pronunciation, due to linguistic changes they underwent. The best way to learn how to write them is by memorization.

A. The initial อย

Written as if it were /ʔy/ but pronounced like a simple /y/, this initial consonant is interpreted as *pre-glottalized y* (/ ʔy/) in old Thai. In the modern language, this sound does not exist any more, yet four very common words are written with this initial consonant. Even though this consonant is now pronounced as simple /y/, it follows the tone rule of initial Mid consonants, apparently because of the historical influence of the, now silent glottal stop.

The only four words that are written with this digraph are:

Table 35: The initial อย

Thai	Phonetic symbol	Meaning
อย่า	yàa	'Do not'
อยู่	yùu	'to live, to stay, to be present'
อย่าง	yàaŋ	'a kind; to be like'
อยาก	yàak	'to want, to crave, to fancy'

B. The lengthened vowels

Table 36 contains words written with short vowels but are **pronounced** with the long vowel counterparts. These nine words are in common everyday use.

119

Table 36: The lengthened vowels

Words	Expected pronunciation	Actual Pronunciation	Meaning
น้ำ	* nám	náam	'water'
ไม้	* máy	máay	'wood'
ได้	* dây	dâay	'to get; to be able'
ใต้	* tây	tâay	'to be under; south'
ไหว้	* wây	wâay [23]	'to greet, to salute in Thai style'
เปล่า	* plàw	plàaw	'no; empty'
เช้า	* cháw	cháaw	'morning'
เก้า	* kâw	kâaw [24]	'nine'
เท้า	* tháw	tháaw	'foot'

[23] This resulted in a pair of homophones: ไหว้ **/wâay/** 'to greet, to salute in Thai style', and ว่าย **/wâay/** 'to swim'.

[24] This also resulted in a pair of homophones: เก้า **/kâaw/** 'nine', and ก้าว **/kâaw/** 'to make a step, to move'.

Exercise 47A

Write the following phrases or sentences in phonetic symbols.

๑. นัก เรียน ไหว้ ครู ตอน เก้า โมง เช้า

_____

๒. ผม อยาก ได้ น้ำ เปล่า ครับ

_____

๓. หนัง สือ อยู่ ที่ ไหน

_____

๔. อย่า พูด อย่าง นั้น

_____

๕. ใต้ ต้น ไม้ มี หญ้า เยอะ

_____

๖. วัน นี้ ว่าย น้ำ ไม่ ได้

_____

Exercise 47B

Write the following phrases or sentences in Thai script.

1. nák rian wâay khruu tɔɔn kâaw mooŋ cháaw

_____

2. phǒm yàak dâay náam plàaw khráp

_____

3. nǎŋ sɯ̌ɯ yùu thîi nǎy

_____

4. yàa phûut yàaŋ nán

_____

5. tâay tôn máay mii yâa yə́

_____

6. wan níi wâay náam mây dâay

_____

C. The short vowels written long.

A considerable number of Thai syllables written with long vowels are pronounced with short vowel when bearing a tone mark. Table 37 contains examples of such words in comparison with the unmarked forms, or the forms with the default tones.

Table 37: Short vowels written long

Words	Expected pronunciation	Actual Pronunciation	Meaning
ทอง	thɔɔŋ	thɔɔŋ	'gold'
ท่อง	* thɔ̂ɔŋ	thɔ̂ŋ	'to memorize'
ตอง	tɔɔŋ	tɔɔŋ	'banana leaf'
ต้อง	* tɔ̂ɔŋ	tɔ̂ŋ	'to have to; to touch'
หอง	hɔ̌ɔŋ	hɔ̌ɔŋ	-
ห้อง	* hɔ̂ɔŋ	hɔ̂ŋ	'room'
แตง	tɛɛŋ	tɛɛŋ	'melon'
แต่ง	* tɛ̀ɛŋ	tɛ̀ŋ	'to decorate; to compose'
แกง	kɛɛŋ	kɛɛŋ	'a Thai dish'; to make such a dish'
แก่ง	* kɛ̀ɛŋ	kɛ̀ŋ	'reef; islet and reef'
แมน	mɛɛn	mɛɛn	'heaven'
แม่น	* mɛ̂ɛn	mɛ̂n	'to be accurate'
เลน	leen	leen	'mire, wet mud'
เล่น	* lêen	lên	'to play'
เกง	keeŋ	keeŋ	-
เก่ง	* kèeŋ	kèŋ	'to be good at'
จอง	cɔɔŋ	cɔɔŋ	'to make a reservation'
จ้อง	* cɔ̂ɔŋ	cɔ̂ŋ	'to stare at'
จ๋อง	* cɔ̌ɔŋ	cɔ̌ŋ	'to be dispirited'
แนว	nɛɛw	nɛɛw	'a streak, a line; a trend'
แน่ว	* nɛ̂ɛw	nɛ̂w	'steadily; firmly'
ปอก	pɔ̀ɔk	pɔ̀ɔk	'to peel'
ป๊อก	* pɔ́ɔk	pɔ́k	'a kind of card game'
เปิน	pəən	pəən	-
เปิ่น	* pə̀ən	pə̀n	'to be awkward'

123

At this point, you must wonder how to write these words in Thai the way they are actually pronounced, i.e. with the sign for short vowels. Table 38 contains examples of such hypothetical forms.

Table 38: CVC with non-default tones

Phonetic symbol	Hypothetical Thai	Actual Thai	Meaning
tôŋ	*เต้าะง > *ตีฺ้อง	ต้อง	'to have to; to touch'
lên	*เล่ะน > *เลี่น	เล่น	'to play'
nɛ̂w	*แน่ะว > *แนี่ว	แน่ว	'steadily; firmly'
pàn	*เป่อะน > *เปีฺ่น	เปิ่น	'to be awkward'

The hypothetical forms present an orthographic problem of writing both ◌ and a tone mark over the same vowel. Seen as less important, the ◌ was then dispensed with.

Thai syllables with short vowel **signs** and tone mark **appear together only** when the vowels are **/a/, /i/, /ɨ/, /u/,** and **/o/.**

Table 39: **/a/, /i/, /ɨ/, /u/, /o/.**

Phonetic symbol	Thai	Meaning
pân	ปั้น	'to mould'
ñĩŋ	นิ่ง	'to be still'
sɨ́ŋ	ซึ้ง	'to be moved, to be touched'
thûŋ	ทุ่ง	'a field'
rôm	ร่ม	'umbrella'

124

Exercise 48A

Write the following words or phrases in phonetic symbols.

๑.   เดน   ————————   ๑๑. แนว หน้า   ————————

๒.   เด่น   ————————   ๑๒. แน่ว แน่   ————————

๓.   กาง เกง   ————————   ๑๓. กระ เตง   ————————

๔.   เก่ง   ————————   ๑๔. กระ เด้ง   ————————

๔.   อ้อน วอน   ————————   ๑๕. ปลอม   ————————

๖.   บิน ว่อน   ————————   ๑๖. ป้อม   ————————

๗.   ปาก บอน   ————————   ๑๗. วาง แผน   ————————

๘.   บ่อน   ————————   ๑๘. แผ่น ดิน   ————————

๙.   ล้น   ————————   ๑๙. ซึม   ————————

๑๐. โล้น   ————————   ๒๐. ปลื้ม   ————————

Exercise 48B

Write the following words or phrases in phonetic symbols.

1. deen _____
2. dèn _____
3. kaaŋ keeŋ _____
4. kèŋ _____
5. ʔɔ̂ɔn wɔɔn _____
6. bin wôn _____
7. pàak bɔɔn _____
8. bɔ̀n _____
9. lɔ́n _____
10. lɔ́ɔn _____

11. nɛɛw nâa _____
12. nêw nɛ̂ɛ _____
13. krà teeŋ _____
14. krà dêŋ _____
15. plɔɔm _____
16. pɔ̂m _____
17. waaŋ phɛ̌ɛn _____
18. phèn din _____
19. sɯm _____
20. plûɯm _____

D. Tone changes.

In rapid speech, some words are pronounced with a tone different from the written form, due to the linguistic changes they underwent. Table 40 contains five such words used regularly.

Table 40: Tone changes

Thai	Careful pronunciation	Rapid pronunciation	Meaning
ฉัน	chǎn	chán	'I, me'
ดิฉัน	dichǎn	dichán	'I, me (female)'
เขา	khǎw	kháw	'he, him; she, her'
ไหม	mǎy	máy	'yes-no question particle'
หนังสือ	nǎŋsɯ̌ɯ	náŋsɯ̌ɯ	'book'

126

E. Tone neutralization.

In rapid speech, if the first syllable in a polysyllabic words is an open syllable with a short vowel, its tone tends to become neutralized; i.e. pronounced with a mid tone. The same phenomenon also happens to a monosyllabic word that is an open syllable with a short vowel in a rapid speech. Table 41 contains examples of such words.

Table 41: Tone neutralization

Thai	Careful pronunciation	Rapid pronunciation	Meaning
ประตู	pràtuu	pratuu	'door'
ดิฉัน	dichǎn	dichán	'I (female)'
อะไร	ʔàray	ʔaray	'what'
บุหรี่	bùřii	buřii	'cigarette'
มะนาว	mánaaw	manaaw	'lemon'
กิโล	kǐloo	kiloo	'kilo'
ละ	lá	la	'each'

Exercise 49 A
Write the following phrases or sentences in phonetic symbols the way they are pronounced in rapid speech.

๑. เขา เปิด ประ ตู ให้ ฉัน

_____

๒. มะม่วง กิโล ละ เท่า ไหร่

_____

๓. เขา ชอบ สูบ บุหรี่ ไหม

_____

๔. เด็ก เด็ก ชอบ กระ โดด โลด เต้น มาก

_____

๕. คืน ฟ้า กระจ่าง ดาว

_____

Exercise 49B

Write the following phrases or sentences in Thai script.

1. kháw pə̀ət pratuu hây chán

   _____

2. ma mûaŋ kiloo la thâwràay

   _____

3. kháw chɔ̂ɔp sùup burìi máy

   _____

4. dèk dèk chɔ̂ɔp kradòot lôot tên mâak

   _____

5. khɯɯn fáa kracàaŋ daaw

   _____

20. Pseudo-Clusters

Pseudo-clusters are two consonant characters that appear immediately next to each other at initial position but do not behave as a cluster. Instead, the first consonant character is pronounced with the 'unwritten', or 'hidden' short vowel /a/ and the second character behaves as the initial consonant of the next syllable. The third important characteristic of syllables with a pseudo-cluster is tone assignment. If the second element of the pseudo-clusters is a sonorant, it will carry the tonal effect of the first consonant through to the vowel. Otherwise, it will behave as an initial consonant of a separate syllable.

The reason for the 'pseudo-cluster' phenomenon is historically. All words exhibiting pseudo-cluster were borrowed from other languages (mostly Khmer) where such two consonants are real cluster.

Table 42: Pseudo-clusters with a sonorant

Thai	Phonetic symbol [25]	Meaning
ขนม	khànǒm	'dessert'
ถนน	thànǒn	'road'
สมุด	sàmùt	'notebook'
สนุก	sànùk	'to be fun'
เสมอ	sàmə̌ə	'always'
สนาม	sànǎam	'lawn, field'
ฉลาด	chàlàat	'to be smart'
แผนก	phànɛ̀ɛk	'department'
ฉลาม	chàlǎam	'shark'
ขยะ	khàyà	'garbage'
สระ	sàrà	'vowel'
อร่อย	ʔàrɔ̀y	'to be delicious'
สแตมป์	satɛɛm	'stamp'

---

[25] Note that in rapid speech, the first syllable in the following words become neutralized.

129

Table 43: Pseudo-clusters without a sonorant

Thai	Phonetic symbol [26]	Meaning
สบาย	sàbaay	'to feel fine, easy'
แสดง	sàdɛɛŋ	'to perform'
สถานี	sàthǎanii	'station'
สตรี	sàtrii	'woman'

Exercise 50A

Write the following sentences in phonetic symbols as they are pronounced in rapid speech.

๑. ห้อง สมุด อยู่ ที่ ถนน อะไร คะ

_____

๒. เขา ไม่ กล้า ว่าย น้ำ ทะ เล เพราะ กลัว ปลา ฉลาม

_____

๓. เด็ก เด็ก ชอบ เล่น ที่ สนาม หญ้า หน้า บ้าน เสมอ

_____

๔. นัก แสดง คน นี้ ฉลาด มาก

_____

๕. ขนม ตก ลง ไป ใน ถัง ขยะ

_____

---

[26] Note that in rapid speech, the tone of the first syllable in these words is neutralized.

Exercise 50B

Write the following sentences in Thai script.

1. hɔ̌ŋ samùt yùu tʰîi thanǒn ʔaray khá

   _____

2. kháw mây klâa wâay náam thalee phrɔ́ klua plaa chalǎam

   _____

3. dèk dèk chɔ̂ɔp lên tʰîi sanǎam yâa nâa bâan samə̌ə

   _____

4. nák sadɛɛŋ khon níi chalàat mâak

   _____

5. khanǒm tòk loŋ pay nay thǎŋ khayà

   _____

Exceptions do exist. Table 44 contains words with initial pseudo-clusters that do not follow the tone assignment rules. There are only few such words and therefore it is not difficult to memorize them.

Table 44: Pseudo-clusters with an exception.

Thai	Expected pronunciation	Actual pronunciation	Meaning
ขโมย	* khàmǒoy	khàmooy	'to steal; thief'
สมาคม	* sàmǎakhom	sàmaakhom	'association, club'
สมาชิก	* sàmǎachík	sàmaachík	'member'
สมาธิ	* sàmǎatʰí	sàmaatʰí	'concentration'

There is also a group of words whose second syllable does not follow tone assignment rules, even though they do not contain a pseudo-cluster. They are listed in Table 45.

131

Table 45: Pseudo pseudo-clusters

Thai	Expected pronunciation	Actual pronunciation	Meaning
ตำรวจ	* tamrûat	tamrùat	'police'
ตำรับ	* tamráp	tamràp	'a formula'
กำเนิด	* kamnə̂ət	kamnə̀ət	'birth'
ประโยค	* pràyôok	pràyòok	'sentence'
ประโยชน์	* pràyôot	pràyòot	'use'
สำเร็จ	* sǎmrét	sǎmrèt	'to succeed'
สำรวจ	* sǎmrûat	sǎmrùat	'to survey'
บุรุษ	* bùrút	bùrùt	'man; person'

Exercise 51A

Write the following sentences in phonetic symbols as they are pronounced in rapid speech.

๑. ตำรวจ กำลัง จับ ขโมย ที่ สนาม บิน

_____

๒. เขา เป็น สมาชิก สมาคม ชม ดาว

_____

๓. ขนม หวาน ไม่ ค่อย มี ประโยชน์ สำหรับ เด็ก และ ผู้ใหญ่

_____

๔. เขา ทำงาน ไม่ ได้ เพราะ ไม่ มี สมาธิ

_____

๕. ประโยค นี้ ยาก ไหม คะ

_____

Exercise 51B

Write the following sentences in Thai script.

1. tamrùat kamlaŋ càp khamooy thîi sanăam bin

_____

2. kháw pen samaachík samaakhom chom daaw

_____

3. khanŏm wăan mây khôy mii prayòot sămràp dèk lɛ́ phûu yày

_____

4. kháw thamŋaan mây dây phrɔ́ mây mii samaathí

_____

5. prayòok níi yâak máy khá

_____

21. Miscellaneous[27]

A. The Irregular a's

Of all the vowel sounds in Thai, the short vowel /a/ seems to be the most versatile one when it comes to writing. So far, we have learned that there are various signs representing this vowel as shown in Table 46:

Table 46: The short vowel /a/

Sound	Sign	Thai	Phonetic symbol	Meaning
a	_ะ	จะ	cà	'will'
a + C (except m, w, y)	_ั_	กัด	kàt	'to bite'
		วัน	wan	'day'
a + m	_ำ	จำ	cam	'to remember'
a + w	เ_า	เรา	raw	'we, us'
a + y	ใ_	ใกล้	klây	'to be near'
	ไ_	ไกล	klay	'to be far'

Even though the six signs for the short vowel /a/ together represent all the possible syllables with /a/ in Modern Thai, there is one more sign used to represent certain syllables whose vowel is **/a/**. These syllables are written with a digraph which looks like two adjacent ร, thus _รร_ . It is called **rɔɔ hǎn**. When not followed by a final consonant, an **/n/** is added to close the syllable. However, this sign can also appear with a written final consonant sign in which case the vowel sign will represent just the vowel **/a/**. Words that are written with **rɔɔ hǎn** are usually of Indic or Khmer origin.

---

[27] This lesson focuses on reading only.

134

Table 47: rɔɔ hǎn

Thai	Phonetic symbol	Meaning
กรรไกร	kankray	'scissors'
บรรจุ	bancù	'to contain, to pack'
บรรทุก	banthúk	'to carry, to load'
กรรม	kam	'act, action, deed/
มรรค	mák	'way'(a religious term)

Finally, a short vowel /a/ can have no written representation at all. This happens in a disyllabic word when the first syllable is a **closed syllable**. In such cases, the final consonant of the preceding syllable also acts as the initial consonant of the unwritten vowel /a/ that follows. Table 48 contains examples of words pronounced with the unwritten /a/

Table 48: The unwritten /a/

Thai	Expected pronunciation	Actual Pronunciation	Meaning
กรรมการ	* kamkaan	kammakaan	'referee'
ภรรยา	* phanyaa	phanrayaa	'wife'
ธรรมดา	* thamdaa	thammadaa	'to be normal'
วิทยุ	* wítyú	wítthayú	'radio'
อิสลาม	* ʔitlaam	ʔitsalaam	'Islam'
อิสระ	* ʔitrá	ʔitsará	'to be free'

135

It is important to review here the consonant signs that have two pronunciations depending on their position in a syllable.

Table 49: Consonants with different pronunciations

Thai	Phonetic symbol	
	Initial	Final
ข ค ฆ	kh	k
จ	c	t
ฉ ช ฌ	ch	t
ซ ศ ษ ส	s	t
ฏ ด	d	t
ฐ ฑ ฒ ถ ท ธ	th	t
บ	b	p
พ ภ	ph	p
ญ	y	n
ล ฬ	l	n
ร	r	n

Exercise 52

Write the following words or phrases in phonetic symbols.

๑. มุสลิม   _____

๒. มหาวิทยาลัย   _____

๓. วรรณกรรม   _____

๔. วรรณคดี   _____

๕. สกปรก   _____

๖. รัฐบาล   _____

๗. บรรพบุรุษ   _____

๘. พรรค   _____

๙. ศาสนา   _____

๑๐. สุขภาพ   _____

B. The Irregular r's

Like the sound and signs for **/a/**, the sound and signs for **/r/** are also complicated to write and pronounce. The complications emerged from **/r/** can be itemized as follows:

1. The unwritten /ɔɔ/

In Lesson 5, we have learned that whenever there are only two consonants and no vowel in a syllable, the unwritten vowel is usually the short vowel **/o/**. However, if the final consonant of such syllables is written with the consonant sign ร the unwritten vowel will be **/ɔɔ/**. Table 50 contains examples of such syllables in comparison with words with the unwritten **/o/**.

137

Table 50: Unwritten **/o/** and **/ɔɔ/**

Thai	Phonetic symbol	Meaning
จน	con	'to be poor; until'
พล	phon	'physical strength'
พร	phɔɔn	'blessing'
กบ	kòp	'frog'
กล	kon	'trick'
กร	kɔɔn	'hand' (royal vocabulary)

We also learned in Lesson 20 that the short vowel **/a/** sound is always inserted between the two consonants of the pseudo-clusters. However, if the second consonant of such clusters is ร, the unwritten, or inserted, vowel sound will **usually** be **/ɔɔ/**, as shown in Table 51.

Table 51: Unwritten **/a/** and **/ɔɔ/** in pseudo clusters

Thai	Phonetic symbol	Meaning
บริษัท	bɔɔrísàt	'a company'
มติ	mátì	'a resolution; an opinion'
มรกต	mɔɔrákòt	'emerald'
กบฏ	kàbòt	'to rebel'
กรณี	kɔɔránii	'a case'

2. The silent ร and **/s/**

A large number of loanwords in Thai were borrowed via written languages. In such cases, while all the signs were transliterated in Thai, not all the sounds may be pronounced, or when they are pronounced in Thai they are pronounced differently, due to the difference in the sound systems of Thai and the donor language.

2.1. Silent ร

The sign ร is usually silent when :

2.1.1. It is the second of two consonant symbols occurring at the end of a syllable. The only common word where this happens is จักร /càk/ 'a disc; a machine'.

2.1.2. It is the first of two consonant symbols written at the end of a syllable.   Examples of such words are: สามารถ /sǎamâat/ 'to be able to', ปรารถนา /pràatthànǎa/ 'to desire'.

2.1.3. It occurs immediately following an initial สร. For example:

Table 52: The initial สร

Thai	Phonetic symbol	Meaning
เสร็จ	sèt	'to finish'
สร้าง	sâaŋ	'to build'
เสริม	sǒəm	'to add, to reinforce'
สระ	sà	'to wash one's hair; a pool'
แสร้ง	sɛ̂ɛŋ	'to pretend'

2.2 . ทร pronounced as /s/

A number of Thai words that were borrowed from Khmer and Sanskrit are spelt with ทร as the initial consonants. The combination /thr/ does not occur in Modern Thai and is replaced by /s/. The tone assignment resulting from the initial /s/ follows that of initial **Low** consonants. Table 53 contains examples of such words.

Table 53: Words with ทร initial.

Thai	Phonetic symbol	Meaning
ทราบ	sâap	'to know'
โทรม	soom	'to be in the state of disrepair'
ทรุด	sút	'to sink, to deteriotate'
กระทรวง	kràsuaŋ	'ministry'
ทรัพยากร	sápphayaakɔɔn	'resource'

139

3. Special sign for /rɯ/, /rɯɯ/, /ri/ and /rəə/

In the Sanskrit vowel system, there is a syllabic **r**, that is an /**r**/ that behaves like a vowel. When words with such vowels were borrowed into Thai via written Sanskrit, the original spelling was kept. As a result we find a number of Thai words with special symbols for the Sanskrit syllabic /**r**/, ฤ (for a short syllabic /**r**/) and ฤๅ (for a long syllabic /**r**/) However, since Thai does not have these sounds, they are replaced by others. ฤ is usually pronounced as /rɯ/, occasionally as /ri/, and in one word as /rəə/. ฤๅ is pronounced as /rɯɯ/. Table 54 contains words with ฤ which are used fairly often in everyday language. Its long counterpart, ฤๅ, can now be found only in old literature.

Table 54: Special sign for /rɯ/, /ri/ and /rəə/

Thai[28]	Phonetic symbol	Meaning
พฤษภาคม	phrɯ́tsàphaakhom	'May'
พฤศจิกายน	phrɯ́tsàcikaayon	'November'
อังกฤษ	ʔaŋkrìt	'England, English'
ฤกษ์	rə̂ək	'an auspicious time'

C. Special sound devices.

1. Vowel shortening mark.

In earlier lessons, we have learned that to write a closed syllable with the short vowel /**e**/ , a special symbol is used to make that effect. This symbol is called ไม้ไต่คู้ /máaytàykhúu/ and looks like a small Thai numeral 8 on top of the initial consonant, as shown in Table 56. Note that even though it is the vowel that is shortened, the shortening mark is written over the initial consonant.

---

[28] Sometimes letters originally intended for use only in Indic loanwords are also used in other words due to historical 'mistakes'.

Table 55 a: Vowel shortening mark

Word	Thai	Meaning
pen	* เ ป ะ น > เป็น	'to be'
rew	* เ ร ะ ว > เร็ว	'to be fast'
dèk	* เ ด ะ ก > เด็ก	'child'
phèt	* เ ผ ะ ด > เผ็ด	'to be spicy'
mét	* เ ม ะ ด > เม็ด	'seed'

We can see from the Table above that another way to derive the spelling of closed syllables with **/e/**, is to say that we just 'shorten' the sign for the long vowel counterpart of **/e/** with ไม้ไต่คู้, as shown in Table 55 b.

Table 55 b: Vowel shortening device

Word	Thai	Meaning
pen	เ ป น > เป็น	'to be'
rew	เ ร ว > เร็ว	'to be fast'
dèk	เ ด ก > เด็ก	'child'
phèt	เ ผ ด > เผ็ด	'to be spicy'
mét	เ ม ด > เม็ด	'seed'

ไม้ไต่คู้ can be used to represent not only the short vowel **/e/**. It can also be used to write **/ɛ/** and **/ɔ/**, as shown in Table 56.

Table 56: ไม้ไต่คู้ [29]

Thai	Phonetic symbol	Meaning
เป็ด	pèt	'duck'
แข็ง	khěŋ	'to be hard'
เซ็ง	seŋ	'to be depressed'
น็อต	nɔ́t	'knot'

_____

[29] Note that the spelling of ก็ /kɔ̂/ 'also, then' is an exception.

141

2. Sound silencers

A large number of Thai words are written with karan (ั)or sound silencer over the final consonant. These are words of foreign origin whose written forms contain consonant combinations that do not exist in Thai. While the Thai writing system tries to preserve the original spelling, the pronunciation is adjusted to suit the Thai phonology. This resulted in one or two consonant sounds being "silenced", or "killed". Examples of such words are shown in Table 57.

Table 57: Words with karan.

Thai	Phonetic symbol	Meaning
อาจารย์	?aacaan	'teacher, professor'
ประโยชน์	pràyòot	'use'
ภูมิศาสตร์	phuumîisàat	'geography'
ศูนย์	sǔun	'center; zero'
แพทย์	phɛ̂ɛt	'medical doctor'
ฟิล์ม	fiim	'film'
การ์ตูน	kaatuun	'cartoon'
มนุษย์	mánút	'human being'
อนุสาวรีย์	?ànùsǎawárii	'monument'
พิพิธภัณฑ์	phíphíttháphan	'museum'
การันต์	karan	'killer mark in Thai writing'

Even though การันต์ /karan/ is responsible for most killings in the Thai writing system, consonants and vowels can also be killed by invisible agents just because they are at the wrong place at the wrong time! The only way to remember how to write words with such ill-fated sounds is by memorization. Note that most of these words are also of foreign origin, and the spelling of them reflects the original forms. Table 58 contains examples of such words.

Table 58: Words with silenced consonants

Thai	Phonetic symbol	Meaning
ไทย	thay	'Thai'
เหตุ	hèet	'cause'
สมบัติ	sǒmbàt	'property'
ประชาธิปไตย	pràchaathíppàtay	'democracy'
พุทธ	phút	'Buddhism'
พราหมณ์	phraam	'Brahman'
เกษตร	kàsèet	'agriculture'
สมัคร	sàmàk	'to apply'
เกียรติ	kǐat	'honour'
ชาติ	châat	'nation'
จริง	ciŋ	'to be true'